T0304093

Employee Communication During Mergers and Acquisitions

To the memory of Cosmo Davenport-Hines 1986–2008

Employee Communication During Mergers and Acquisitions

JENNY DAVENPORT AND
SIMON BARROW

Routledge
Taylor & Francis Group

LONDON AND NEW YORK

First published 2009 by Gower Publishing

Published 2016 by Routledge
2 Park Square, Milton Park, Abingdon, Oxon OX14 4RN
711 Third Avenue, New York, NY 10017, USA

Routledge is an imprint of the Taylor & Francis Group, an informa business

British Library Cataloguing in Publication Data
Davenport, Jenny
  Employee communication during mergers and acquisitions
  1. Communication in industrial relations 2. Consolidation
  and merger of corporations
  I. Title II. Barrow, Simon
  658.3'15

  ISBN 9780566086380 (hbk)

Library of Congress Control Number
Davenport, Jenny.
  Employee communication during mergers and acquisitions / by Jenny Davenport
  and Simon Barrow.
    p. cm.
  Includes bibliographical references and index.
  ISBN 978-0-566-08638-0 (hardcover) 1. Communication in personnel
  management--United States. 2. Consolidation and merger of corporations--
  United States. I. Barrow, Simon. II. Title.
  HF5549.5.C6D27 2008
  658.1'62014--dc22

                                                                    2008043808

Contents

List of Figures

List of Tables

Acknowledgements

This book has been a long time in the writing and we are grateful to a number of people for their help and patience in the long gestation.

First of all, we would like to thank the interviewees, many of whom chose to remain anonymous, but others who gave information about their current or previous employers include Colin Archer, Martin Bishop, Heather Davies, John Doughty, Nigel Edwards, Linda Fay, Bob Griffin, Kevin Hawkins, Morag Holding, Yvonne Hunt, Elaine Macfarlane, Dorothy Macrow, Maria Mahon, Karen Martin, Emma Oliver, Stephen Pain, Mike Pemberton, David Salter, Jacky Simmonds, Jon Weedon and Paul Williams. And many others in focus groups or casual conversations.

We would also like to thank our various colleagues over the years, particularly Liz Cochrane, Richard Mosley, Sir Thomas Boyd-Carpenter and Amy Pike, and our endlessly patient assistant commissioning editor Fiona Martin.

Jenny Davenport and Simon Barrow

Foreword by Simon Robertson

M̲y background is primarily as an investment banker, but I am also a non-executive director and a company chairman. While leaders must be good communicators, I defer to others on the art of good communication. Why am I therefore happy to write a short foreword to a book on communication?

The answer lies in my belief that transparent and honest communications are key to successful mergers and acquisitions, not only in getting any deal completed but more importantly in making any merger or acquisition successful over the long term.

Any adviser or company executive who has been as closely involved as I have will know the immense corporate and personal pressures that dominate life during such periods. It is a time which tests everyone's fortitude, conviction, diplomacy, loyalty, energy and professional ability. That is because, like other moments of great change, the stakes are very high – a lifetime's work potentially lost, a vision ended and a team destroyed. Equally, behind a public front to build one great coherent group may lie individuals whose personal interests are very different. Overall, there is, for some, the potential for substantial personal gain and for others a lifetime of commitment shattered.

In the pressure to get the deals "done", all too often good internal communications are left behind. First, the strictures of dealing with price sensitive information result in severe restrictions on the full dissemination of information. Secondly, the advisers are primarily concerned in ensuring the deal gets completed within the requirements of the regulations but also unfortunately as their remuneration is too biased towards success. And thirdly and perhaps as importantly, senior managements' time is focused on the deal and their own position and not sufficiently on leading and inspiring the business.

This book should therefore prove invaluable to people in the communications industry who work with Chief Executives and senior managers who have the responsibility of ensuring that mergers and acquisitions happen as seamlessly as possible and crucially the integration of the businesses result in the new group being stronger than the two companies were before the transaction. What I hope this excellent book will do is to help everybody who is concerned with communications before, during and after mergers and acquisitions understand that effective and transparent communications adds enormous value to the end result. And conversely sub-standard communications can be extremely damaging.

SIMON ROBERTSON

Simon Robertson has been an investment banker for over 40 years and has advised on many substantial mergers and acquisitions. He has been Chairman of Rolls-Royce plc since 2005 and is also a non-executive director of HSBC Holdings plc, Berry Bros & Rudd Ltd, The Economist Newspaper Limited, the Royal Opera House and The Eden Project. He started his own corporate advisory business Simon Robertson Associates in 2006. He was formerly the president of Goldman Sachs Europe and Chairman of Kleinwort Benson plc.

Introduction

The rate of failure of mergers and acquisitions (M&A) has been variously estimated at anything between 50 and 75 per cent. A McKinsey study in the early 1980s found that over a 10-year period only 23 per cent of acquisitions recovered the cost incurred during the acquisition and for 66 per cent of acquirers they would have earned a greater return in a bank savings account. (Magnet 1984). More recently, a KPMG survey in 2001 found that 70 per cent of M&A combinations failed to add value.

Much has been written about the failure rates in M&A and the reasons for the failure. However, taking into account the huge communication and cultural challenges of a merger or acquisition, it is perhaps surprising that so many succeed.

People's work is important to them. It provides them not only with their income but a large part of their social identity. Work provides them (usually) with companionship, and even friendship, and is where people learn new skills and experiment with new ways of doing things and relating to people. In recent years, as organisations have woken up to the importance of harnessing their employees' commitment, people have been encouraged to identify themselves not merely with their immediate workteams but ever further with their organisations and the brands they deliver or sell.

When an organisation changes its identity by merger or acquisition, this problem strikes at the heart of the identity and loyalty that people have built up for their organisation. This identity has often been developed at considerable cost and effort by an organisation consciously building an employer brand which enables them to attract, retain and motivate the people they need. Managers and professionals in particular have been urged to donate their discretionary effort to the organisation as a cause which they can feel proud to be part of. It is hardly surprising, then, that for many people the news that the entity which employs them is to cease to exist is painful news. There is an emotional connection which goes beyond a purely transactional relationship with the employer.

Your employer is part of your identity, not just for social definition, but for your CV. Having a great employer brand in your history is useful all your working life, like having been to a great university. The destruction of an employer brand is potentially a loss not simply of identity but also of value, as future employers cease to recognise or value the name of the former organisation.

People can therefore understandably resent those who made the decisions – inevitably in secret – which have deprived them of the organisation they identified with. Imagine if the Prime Minister of the UK made a secret deal to merge the country with France. The reasons might be excellent, but many people would feel resentful and betrayed, even if they acknowledged the logic.

There are also often perfectly rational fears about job security, career advancement and ongoing levels of benefits associated with a merger or acquisition. Often, the more senior the person, the more threatened they are by these realistic fears.

This, then, is the emotional climate in which much of the internal communicator's work must be done. Often the natural leaders and communicators are those who had the largest stake, financially or emotionally, in the old regime. These are the people to whom others will listen.

To make their jobs harder, internal communication specialists are sometimes not insiders at the time of negotiation and have little or no notice when they are asked to communicate the merger or acquisition. Then they find that every word they want to say is pored over by lawyers, hampering speed and clear language of communication, which communicators know to be essential. Often there are political considerations too, as different members of the senior team wish to give a different spin on decisions.

WHAT THIS BOOK IS FOR

Much has been written about the role of human resource professionals in M&A, especially in a stream of excellent publications from executive education and research provider Roffey Park. Less, however, has been said about the role of internal communicators. Although the books always stress the importance of communication, there is little detail about what to do when, and how to overcome, or at least minimise, the practical problems inherent in trying to communicate at a time when there is often little news and when so much must remain confidential. This book is an attempt to meet that need, with checklists, examples and tables to help busy communicators who do not want to have to make more experiments than they need at such a vital time.

It covers a range of M&A types, from the so-called merger of equals to the acquisition of an organisation of a very different size, and even the sale or acquisition of parts of an organisation such as one division or factory. It is also relevant to the outsourcing of departments. Although the legal implications are different in these varying scenarios, for the people employed in them the issues are similar, namely the loss of identity of an old organisation and the joining together with people from another organisation. It is these issues of identity and working with new people and processes that this book hopes to address.

In addition to the text and tables, examples from case studies are given throughout. In many cases the organisations cannot be named, as they have given information on the understanding that it will inform the book but not identify them. Where possible, though, and especially for the more successful examples, we quote the organisation and our source. We also include real quotations from employees at the varying stages of the process.

AN OVERVIEW OF THE MERGERS AND ACQUISITIONS PROCESS

The M&A process can be divided into clear stages, each with its own challenges and opportunities to help the merger succeed. This is the timeline for M&As which will be used as the structure for this book:

Stage One: The strategic need and identifying the partner.

Stage Two: Due diligence.

Stage Three: Preparing for and making the initial announcement.

Stage Four: Between announcement and Day One.

Stage Five: The first 100 days.

Stage Six: Establishing the new employer brand.

In practice the work that is done in the various stages varies considerably. Where there is a friendly acquisition much of the work relating to the first 100 days can be done alongside the due diligence, so that there is an almost seamless transfer from investigation to planning. In cases where regulatory requirements cause a long delay between announcement and the actual merger, as with the GlaxoWellcome–SmithKline Beecham merger for example, there can also be an opportunity for much of the detailed planning often done in the first 100 days to take place before the actual merger.

In giving this outline then, we would advise that communicators should look at the chapters before and after the one they are immediately concerned with, as the work being done may be happening at a different stage in their deal from the process described in this book.

We know that the world around the organisation does not stop while it gets on quietly with its integration, and that in many cases the communication of the merger or acquisition is happening at the same time as other challenging communication projects. This, of course, makes the story of merger communication much more complicated. We shall see this particularly in the case studies of GlaxoSmithKline and Aviva.

We are also aware that in many cases the integration projects go on for much longer than the first 100 days. However, with the ongoing pace of change in organisations and the constant projects to create improvements or cut costs, even in business as usual, we are going to cover ongoing integration projects as part of the building of the new organisation.

Each of these stages has its own key players who will be driving the deal or facilitating integration; communicators need to establish relationships with all of them at different stages and it is helpful if they can understand the drivers that motivate these people.

Each chapter contains for its stage of the process:

- Practical advice on issues to address.

- Key internal players – who are they and what are their preoccupations?

- What sort of listening you need to do.

- What employees are thinking and saying.

- The cost of getting it wrong.

- Stories from anonymous or quoted real-life case studies.

- A summary of your priorities for this stage.

DIFFERENT MODELS OF MERGERS AND ACQUISITIONS

Mergers and acquisitions have different aims and people hold different organisational models in their heads about the potential new organisation. The model chosen depends partly on the fundamental reasons for the deal. We will look at various rationales in more detail in Stage One; the aim here is to give an idea of the range of challenges a communicator faces, depending on the degree of integration which is planned.

At one extreme, the two organisations may continue pretty much exactly as before, with no changes to operations, customer relations or to management, but simply some changes in the financial reporting arrangements. At the other extreme, the new management will be looking to integrate the organisations completely to create a totally new organisation, so that after a while no one will remember who used to work for which of the former parts.

There are four commonly accepted alternatives in terms of integration, each of which can have an infinite number of variations:

1. Preservation of the old ways in each organisation. In practice there are likely to be some changes in financial reporting arrangements, if nothing else. This is most likely to be the case where the acquirer has little knowledge of the market or technology that the target has, and trusts the former management to continue, perhaps taking advantage of some of the parent company's own customer base or technology. This is obviously the case where the acquisition is by a holding company, and is often stated to be the case when buying owner-managed firms where the former owners continue to manage the old enterprise, often in an earn-out over several years.

2. Assimilation of the target into the new parent. This is particularly common when the target is very much smaller than the parent, and when the work it does is similar to that of the parent company. This is typically the case with a "serial acquirer", which buys up a range of similar small businesses, sometimes just to obtain a particular piece of technology, and assimilates the company into the new one. It would also apply to outsourcing where a company wins a contract to do the work previously done in-house and former employees transfer to the outsourcing company.

3. Integration attempting to use the "best of both" from the old and new organisations. The plan here is to have a single new company but for neither of the organisations automatically to dominate the new entity. This is typically the case with mergers or acquisitions of organisations of similar sizes. In practice this is perhaps the hardest type of integration to realise successfully, since there is a tendency for one organisation to dominate the other as the integration progresses. GlaxoSmithKline (GSK) is one of few success stories of this kind.

4. The creation of a completely new company which, while honouring the traditions of the old ones, attempts explicitly to create a new one, often creating a new name unlike either of the old names and deliberately setting out to create its own culture and values. Financial services group Aviva is an example of this.

The extent to which the new organisation will be looking for integration will depend on the reasons for the acquisition, with integration being more likely if the companies are doing similar business and functions can be shared and costs cut, or if there are overlaps between the two organisations.
All this will impact on the amount and types of communication required (See Table I.1).

Table I.1   Overview of communication needs in different sorts of mergers and acquisitions

	Target is much smaller than bidder	Target is nearly as big, bigger or the same size
Little integration planned	• Little communication necessary in the bidder. • Most communication in target can be left to local management with some reassuring messages from the centre. • Rationale for not integrating must be repeated again and again.	• There will be considerable concern in both parties, and communication will need to be consistent across the parties even though there is little integration planned, as there is bound to be informal communication across the companies and people will be looking for news. • Rationale for not integrating must be repeated again and again; people will be reluctant to believe it.
Much integration planned	• There must be much more communication from the bidder to the target's people.	• The biggest communication challenge. Everyone will anticipate change and some will fear it. • There will be a great thirst for communication.

There may of course be no intention of keeping many or indeed any of the target's employees. The acquisition may be purely a way of buying a patent or other rights. If this is the case most of this book will not be relevant to you.

HOW POOR COMMUNICATION AND MISUNDERSTANDING OF CULTURAL DIFFERENCES CAN DESTROY VALUE IN INTEGRATION

It is widely accepted that failure to manage cultural differences is a primary reason that M&As fail. A 1996 survey in the US of chief financial officers listed incompatible cultures as the number one pitfall (Bureau of Business Research at American International College, Springfield MA, reported in *CFO Magazine* April 1996). As we describe the various stages we will show the particular pitfalls and how failure to manage communication and culture costs value.

WHAT CAN COMMUNICATORS DO TO ENSURE THAT THEY ARE IN THE BEST POSSIBLE POSITION TO HELP?

As we have noted, internal communicators are often late to know about a pending acquisition. How soon you know often depends on where you sit in the organisation, both in terms of seniority and in which department, as we will discuss later. Wherever you sit, there are things you can do to make sure that you are involved early in the process, and that your opinion will be valued:

1. be prepared for an announcement if it is clear from the strategy or from industry consolidation that a deal of some sort is likely;

2. know what the process is likely to be when it does come;

3. know who the key players are likely to be;

4. ensure that they know what help the internal communicator can be;

5. ensure that you know within your own organisation how communication really works and how to reach or tap into the various audiences within it.

WHERE SHOULD THE INTERNAL COMMUNICATION FUNCTION SIT?

Internal communication professionals can belong in various parts of the organisation. There are advantages wherever one sits, and there is no one right place to be. It will depend on what the strategy and priorities for the organisation are, and who within the top team is both influential and cares about internal communication. The important thing is to have a sponsor at the top table who values internal communication *and* is privy to the key decisions throughout the process.

Potential Advantages of Being in Corporate Communication, Public Affairs or Public Relations

*   The director of corporate communication is usually an insider very early on in the process, as directors tend to know that they will need the support of shareholders and of the press, even if they have not thought through the internal communication implications.

*   It is hugely helpful to be able to plan the communication strategies to the various stakeholders together. There is a wide overlap of audiences: shareholders read the papers, some employees are

shareholders, customers talk to employees, and so on. Even though each audience needs planning for distinctly (see Stage Two for details), it is important that the key messages are consistent across all the stakeholders.

- The skills of mass communication, including the use of technology and the actual wording of messages, are most likely to be sophisticated within the corporate communication function.

Potential Advantages of Being in Human Resources

- Human resources professionals usually understand the range of employees and their varying levels of knowledge and attitudes.

- In HR it is easier to link communication training with other development initiatives.

- Colleagues in HR understand the union or other employee representative structures and the key personalities within them.

- Managing culture is usually understood to be within the realm of HR so it will normally be easier to assess and drive culture from HR.

- Many of the concerns people will have, such as their pay, career prospects and pension, are answered by information emanating from HR. It is useful to be able to plan communication across both business and personal topics.

Potential Advantages of Being in Marketing

- Marketing departments are close to the customers and their understanding of the brand, so internal communication based in marketing never drifts too far from the need to continue to meet customers' needs.

- Knowledge of how to run large events for employees, engaging emotions as well as intellect, usually rests with the marketing function.

- When it comes to creating the employer brand of the new organisation, the marketing department's knowledge is essential, since they understand brands and how to create them.

Potential Advantages of Working Directly for the Chief Executive

- Working for the chief executive gives you immediate access to up-to-date information.

- A communication professional working directly for the CEO usually carries "clout" and can get things done by using the CEO's name.

In practice wherever the internal communication professional sits he or she will need to have allies and colleagues in the other disciplines and will need to work closely with them throughout the process.

ROLE OF COMMUNICATION SPECIALISTS IN A MERGER OR ACQUISITION

Senior communication advisers have a role in helping leaders of the organisation frame their communications to the various important audiences, both internal and external. In our view they have another important role, which arises from their closeness to these various stakeholders: an ability to representing the stakeholders' likely views and reactions to the organisation's leaders. This position also gives them the opportunity to ask questions with a pseudo external voice. It means that they can in some ways play the role of devil's advocate and ask the simple and big questions at a time when the rest of the leadership team may be supporting each other in a "groupthink" way, avoiding potential conflict within the team by failing to expose shortcomings in arguments or holes in assumptions.

The communicator can also be extremely helpful to the senior people, the more so the earlier they are involved. They can take considerable work (in terms of drafting and responding to questions) away from the top team at a time when the top team themselves will be desperately overloaded. In order for leaders to delegate these communication tasks to their professionals they must trust them completely and be confident that they know the full story.

It is also part of the communicator's role to make sure that there is a coherent story explaining the need for the deal and the benefits of it. This needs to include marshalling the evidence and the creation of a narrative which can be told in various length versions according to the audience. It is important that this is essentially a single story, although different parts of the evidence and lessons may be stressed for different audiences at different stages of the process. This is primarily the role of the senior communication executive in the business, but it is useful for the internal communicator to have a role in helping to construct the story, to check that the evidence will make sense to internal as well as external audiences.

With an internal focus, you need to make sure that the actions of leaders match their words. Employees in both bidder and target organisations will watch the leaders carefully and attempt to read things into every movement and action as well as into every phrase that they utter. As communicators you need to be aware of this and to make sure the leaders also understand it. There are, of course, implications about how and what you can communicate. You are constrained by the real personality and priorities of the leaders of the new enterprise. There is no point inventing a good story if it is undermined in practice by the tone, words or actions of the leadership. It is better to have a *consistent* story, even if it is less attractive than the one you would like to tell.

THEMES OF INTERNAL COMMUNICATION THROUGHOUT THE PERIOD OF ACQUISITION AND INTO THE FORMATION OF THE NEW ORGANISATION

The content of the communication of course varies according to the story that needs telling. There are also different sorts of communication needed at the different stages, as we will explain throughout the book.

Table 1.2   Different sorts of communication needed at different stages of a merger or acquisition

Stage	Communication to workforce	Sort of listening needed
Prior to specific deal	• Commercial realities in the industry. • How and why things will go quiet when a deal is in sight.	• Current fears and rumours.
Due diligence	• Usually none.	• None overt usually.
Announcement	• Quick communication to beat the public media. • Main messages must be consistent with other audiences and clear.	• Current fears and rumours. • Reactions to the announcement. • Workforce's current knowledge and views of merger partner.
Between announcement and completion	• Why there is so little to be said. • Timetable and process. • May be able to start making announcements about structure and strategy.	• Current fears and rumours. • Representatives' views about the proposed deal.
Day One	• Main messages (still and again). • Initial decisions and reasons for them. • Timetable and process. • How people will be involved. • How individuals will be affected.	• Current fears and rumours. • Channels for individual concerns.
First 100 days	• As before PLUS detail as it becomes available. • Beware of overload.	• Involved in detailed decision-making with clear roles.
Building the ongoing business	• Mission vision and values of new organisation.	• Involved in creating the new organisation.

SUMMARY OF COMMUNICATION NEEDS AT VARIOUS STAGES

In addition to the varying communication needs implied here there are a number of essential ongoing themes. One is the need for people to feel valued. This has a number of components. People need to feel:

- my previous career and the work and effort I have put in over many years have not been forgotten, whatever the future holds for me;

- the organisation cares about me and my future, even if there is not a place for me in the new organisation;

- I will be treated with respect in that I will personally be told information relating to me as soon as practicable, and I will not expect to hear from a third party;

- there is always someone with the time to listen to my concerns and fears.

As long as the communicator bears these in mind – for all categories of employee at all stages of the process – they cannot go too far wrong.

SUMMARY OF COMMUNICATION NEEDS AT VARIOUS STAGES

1 Stage One: The Strategic Need – Before a Partner is Identified

In this chapter we introduce the rationale and emotional background to the deal, so you as the communicator can understand top management's processes in the early stages before a partner has been found. Next we look specifically at the communication challenges at this stage: your work with the top team; communication of long-term strategy; and ensuring that your communication channels are up-to-date and functional. The chapter will end with sections on key players, what employees are thinking and saying, the sorts of listening you need to do at this stage and the cost of getting it wrong.

THE EMOTIONAL BACKGROUND TO A DEAL

One of the ways that emotions underpin mergers and acquisitions is in the often unacknowledged importance of the chemistry at the top. In Hunt's 1987 study for London Business School 31 per cent of his sample admitted that the major motivation for a merger or acquisition was personal or political rather than strategic. At some stage at the beginning of the process senior people meet, however informally, to start discussing the possibility of the deal. It seems that personal regard for, or a perceived ability to work with, the other party is often central to the deal going forward. In one case we know of, a target was identified quite early on and rejected after an intense, early due diligence process. The deal was, however, subsequently signed following a game of golf between the target owner and the bidder's chairman.

Once a target is identified there is also a momentum which builds up from the advisers, which makes it psychologically hard to retreat. Many of the advisers during a merger or acquisition will earn more if the deal goes through. For others it is better for their CV to record their work on a deal than went through than on an abortive one. In other words, for most of your advisers it will be in their interest to see the deal through; they are unlikely to advise against it unless the case for pulling out is very strong. Once you have engaged advisers it can be hard to pull back. It is therefore essential that before a potential partner is identified, the acquisition team is clear about what are the required and desirable features of the potential target and what contra-indications would deter them.

Psychologically for the top team, too, it can be hard to draw back. For the target, especially if top management have publicly supported the deal, there is a danger that it can seem that the organisation is "in play" and that the current management team does not have the appetite to continue to run the company itself. For the bidder there may be a sense of having been thwarted in the execution of its strategy, itself a potential threat to the reputation of the current management. For both sides there will be a feeling that much time and energy, which could have been devoted to other activities, has been expended on a fruitless venture. Avoiding the pain of this waste can sometimes drive people to continue with deals even while part of them knows it is not the right thing for the organisation, and the deal goes ahead. All the more reason, then, to be absolutely clear about why you are looking for an acquisition rather than organic growth. The communicator can have a role in helping the top team think through the implications, in communication and reputation terms, of going for an acquisition strategy which falls through.

POSSIBLE REASONS FOR ACQUISITIONS

It is not the purpose of this book to cover strategy. However, in order to provide some context for the decisions about the deal, we list here the main strategic reasons why organisations embark on a strategy of acquisition. It is useful for the communicator to be able to convey these alternative reasons as part of the general education of the workforce in advance of the sighting of a specific target.

Typical reasons for an acquisition:

- To strengthen the organisation's competitive position by building new capabilities or adding resources to existing businesses. This may be by moving into similar businesses in new areas geographically or by moving into a new technology, sometimes eliminating reliance on another party in the supply chain.

- To increase sales volume.

- To capitalise on opportunities by reducing costs through adding technology, eliminating overlaps and/or achieving economies of scale.

There are many such lists in the literature, with the various rational reasons for a deal. Marion Devine (2002) lists some of the less public or respectable reasons why companies *really* go for mergers or acquisitions. As the communicator, you need to be aware of which, if any, of these factors have influenced the top teams in your deal, so you can be prepared if they are rumbled by some of your canny internal audience. Devine's list:

1.   quest for bigness;

2.   saving face (promised turnover of a certain amount by a certain date);

3.   short-term pressure;

4.   boredom;

5.   fear of being left on the shelf;

6.   copying other people in the sector;

7.   CEO hubris (Columbia University found a correlation between CEO ego and low value extracted from acquisitions they made).

Sometimes acquisitions are driven by more negative forces: a need to acquire an organisation in order to prevent competitors from buying it and reaping competitive advantages, or the need to buy to make your organisation too big for a bigger predator to snatch up.

Clarity of Vision about the Purpose of the Merger or Acquisition

Many of the problems of losing value in integration can be put down to lack of clarity or variety of views about the purpose of the deal. As with any other major strategic development there is always a danger that there is no real agreement behind a form or words to which all can adhere. Employer brand consultancy People in Business is often called in when an organisation is experiencing problems with integration. Our work usually includes individual interviews with the key players and sometimes reveals that there was no real common understanding of the strategic imperatives behind the acquisition. Too often there are, in fact, quite different aspirations for the deal, which each imply a different way of running the new organisation.

The problem often arises at the level of language. People use the same words but mean different things. As the language adviser, the communication specialist needs to ensure that there is some common meaning under the common words. The best time to have these conversations is before an actual target has been identified so that emotions have not yet clouded judgement to quite the extent that they may do once personalities are involved.

The communicator has three roles before a merger partner, potential buyer or acquisition target has been announced:

1.   attempting to ensure that the top team really are thinking along the same lines;

2.   ensuring that there is managed communication rather than rumour or contradictory stories about the strategic situation;

3. ensuring that your communication channels are up-to-date and functional.

We will look at each of these in turn.

ENSURING THERE IS REAL COMMON UNDERSTANDING AMONG THE TOP TEAM

*   Ask each member of the board or key acquisition team individually to write down the three top reasons for the acquisition and what they see the new organisation or two organisations looking like in a year's time.

*   Ask them to give examples of what they mean in real terms, such as relations with suppliers or customers, when they lapse into management jargon.

*   Ask them to talk through moments of truth where value is created in the organisation.

*   Present the findings back to the teams and make sure that the disagreements are fully thrashed out.

Once There is a Potential Target

There is usually some due diligence conducted even before approaching the target or entering full negotiations. Obviously, much of the work at this stage is on the commercial elements of the deal. There are three main concerns for the communicator. If a high degree of integration is sought the acquirer will need to be confident that:

*   the culture of the target is not so far from that of the bidder that integration will be long and expensive;

*   communication structures are in place which are credible and efficacious so that the early communication of the deal, which will be in the hands of the target's management, does not poison people against the deal or cause so much worry that key employees choose to look elsewhere for work;

*   there is a readiness for change in both parties.

The acquirer also needs to consider to what extent previous mergers, acquisitions or other major structural changes have been digested. This can be a problem in either the target or the bidder. Not only will this influence the amount of ongoing work needed in projects and so on, with all the attendant potential disruption for customers, but it will dictate the soundtrack that is playing in people's heads before a word is communicated about a new prospective deal. If it went badly, would it be possible to distinguish a new deal sufficiently for it not to be tarred with the same brush? If, therefore, either party to the potential deal has recently been through a merger it is worth checking how the deal is thought of within the company and to what extent there are still integration projects continuing.

In advance of seeking a potential partner it can also be helpful to benchmark key aspects of the operation so that the due diligence team knows what sort of standards they should be looking for.

See Chapter 2: Stage Two for more information about due diligence.

Explaining the Future Silence

There are some very practical things that need communicating now, especially to senior people. In particular you should explain that the process of making a deal will have to be shrouded in secrecy as soon as a target is in sight. Only those who absolutely need to know will do so, so people are likely to feel out of the loop as others disappear to hotels or advisers' venues. They need to understand that this is not a personal slight. Others in the organisation need to know that things will go very quiet once a deal is in sight, and that the first they will know of it is when there is an announcement of a statement of intent. This is not a failure of communication or lack of respect to the workforce; it is simply how this sort of deal is done.

ENSURING THERE IS EFFECTIVE COMMUNICATION ABOUT THE STRATEGIC SITUATION

Typically the first and main audiences for the strategic plans of the organisation are the City, your bankers and analysts. Investor relations communication specialists may be leading this communication. However, it is also important that you consider the internal audience and the audience of potential employees at this stage, too. If the organisation is a plc, it is likely that at least some of your employees are shareholders and read the annual report carefully for any hints about future strategic direction. Articles in the financial press will also be pored over in kitchens and over cups of coffee around the organisation; people will be talking about possible mergers, with varying degrees of ignorance and worry. There are two key tasks for the internal communicator at this time: to offer a coherent story about how the organisation sees its future and to explain to people the silence that will come about if ever a specific deal is in the frame.

Even if there is no deal envisaged, there is much to be said for internal clarity about the strategy the organisation is seeking to follow. In particular it can be helpful if you can enlist employees in the organisation's noble purpose, such as the value of the goods and services. In the pharmaceutical industry, for example, organisations can stress the value of their products in curing illnesses and helping people to lead pain-free lives. GlaxoSmithKline's mission, which features prominently on its sites and in its literature, is "Do more, feel better, live longer". It helps people justify their working lives, and the often uncomfortable hours they may have to work, if they can feel that there is good resulting from it. This justification may be important both to themselves and to their friends and family.

Every organisation has some sort of story about the positive impact it makes on the world, even if it is only on the employees and the organisation's suppliers. Usually there is more, as the organisation helps some group of people with some aspect of their lives. It is part of the communicator's job to identify this higher aim. Even in its absence employees prefer to engage with an enterprise than merely to do their jobs. Bill Quirke (2000) cites the fact that 84 per cent of employees who understand what makes their business successful want to help create that success, whereas only 46 per cent of those who do not understand share that feeling.

How to Communicate Strategy to Employees

Communicating strategy is a quite different challenge from the more usual process of communicating an event or a decision. There is not the same time pressure, so it is possible to communicate in a more leisurely and engaging way. However, it is not easy to communicate, as employees' previous knowledge or preconceptions vary and hence their understanding of any messages you send out will also be varied. The evidence suggests that communication of strategy is often unsuccessful. In a survey of Fortune 50 companies, 82 per cent of the executives believed that the corporate strategy was understood by all who needed to, while Bill Quirke quotes a Louis Harris survey which found fewer than a third of employees agreeing that "management provides clear goals and direction".

There are two important elements in the successful communication of strategy:

1. The need to tell a convincing story. People think in stories and remember stories. Stories rather than lists of facts or reasons are how our minds work. We naturally try to select and organise facts in order to make a story. If the company does not tell a story itself, employees will make up their own versions.

2. The need to engage people in thinking through the strategy for themselves.

The Elements of a Good Story

There are a number of elements that make up a convincing story:

*   *Context*: "Once upon a time ... ", the traditional beginning of a story, tells you where and when the story is to take place. Make sure the

context setting is not missing from internal communication. Do not assume that employees have the same version of factors facing the company as the leaders of the enterprise. The best house newspapers now carry as much information about the industry and issues facing it as they do about the company's own activities. While employees themselves naturally have sources about the industry and economy, from their reading of general and specific media, they are unlikely to have come to the same conclusions. The company needs to have its own version of what is happening, which should cover:

— The history of the company, what its mistakes were and to what it owes its success. This is an important part of a shared view of what the company is. One version or another will be in the heads of everyone in the organisation, learned from colleagues or from a formal induction. It is the context into which people will hear future plans and changes.

— The regulatory environment and what direction this is moving in.

— Changes in technology or other inventions or discoveries affecting and likely to affect the organisation.

— Changes in the marketplace caused by changes in society or by changes in customer buying patterns.

— Likely moves of competitors or suppliers and the implications for the company.

It is important not to be overtly party political if possible, as that naturally generates opposing views among those who do not share the leaders' political views:

• *Choice*: In order to have an element of drama, there need to be moments of truth in the story where the hero (or the company) has to make a choice about which way to go forward. This is both a part of understanding the history and a way of understanding the current strategy. If people understand that the company reached its current state as a result of choices at different stages they will see how open the options are for the company now. At certain stages in its history it had a choice about whether to invest in a certain technology, or expand into a certain market or do a deal with a certain supplier. At all of these stages there were alternatives which could have led the company down another path. On the verge of a potential acquisition or merger there are again choices, which the current leadership will make to the best of its ability, but the outcome is not pre-ordained. Talking about choices is an important way of treating employees as adults and preventing them from sinking into an infantilised way of looking at the company as if it is all-powerful.

- *A moral*: In a story things that happen are Good or Bad. In the same way, communication within an organisation needs meaning. It is not enough merely to state facts. There needs to be some interpretation of the implications for the organisation so that employees can make sense of it. While people may be wary of "spin" they still expect to see the company having a coherent version of events.

Of course, the company's version is only one of an infinite variety of stories which could be truthfully told by selecting different facts or interpreting them in another way. There are bound to be other stories competing with yours. It is therefore important that yours is well told, explaining why you have chosen the facts and interpretation that you have and why alternative versions are inferior.

20

In order to engage people in the strategy, employees need to be encouraged to think the strategy through for themselves. Explaining it in the context of a story helps, since it enables the thinking behind the strategy to be transparent. It is better still if they think the stages through for themselves, by being given time in planned sessions to examine alternatives.

Engagement through a realistic business game

One large manufacturing organisation, realising that it faced huge cost competition from the Far East, ran sessions for employees, giving them facts about costs and setting people a puzzle in the form of a business game to think through what options were available. When there were subsequent changes in organisation and structure on the shop floor people did not have to have the strategy explained to them from scratch, as they had reached most of the conclusions already for themselves.

Induction and Re-induction

It is important to communicate the strategic position of the organisation to new employees in their first few months in the organisation. Many organisations have put enormous effort into developing excellent induction programmes which explain the drivers for business success, showing new employees who the organisation's customers are and why they choose this organisation over others, and talking about the features needed for ongoing success. These induction programmes often take place over one or more days, giving participants a chance to think the implications through for themselves, often including games or exercises.

A number of companies are now making the investment in running similar exercises for employees on a regular basis, recognising that the competitive environment for the organisation is constantly changing and that employees need to feel up-to-date and engaged with the current position. Half a day at least gives the organisation a chance to run the sort of interactive session that enables people to think things through more than they could simply by reading or listening to a presentation.

Trust

Any subsequent communication, once a deal has been agreed, is considerably easier if there is already a relationship of trust. No communication ever falls into a vacuum in people's heads. There is always some mindset into which people will put new data; if there is not they simply cannot take it in. Investing in a relationship where people understand the strategic challenges facing the company pays dividends at a time such as a merger, when there is a great deal of new information to give them.

Trust is an elusive but useful element in relations with employees. It has various odd characteristics:

- It comprises two rather different dimensions: competence and honesty. A top management team can be trusted as competent operators who know what they are doing, but distrusted as people who are only out for their own ends and care nothing for the future of the company or the people working in it. Alternatively the top team can be seen as decent people, but fundamentally not up to the strategic challenge. It is worth being aware that you need to give cause for trust in both dimensions.

- Trust takes time to build and can be quickly lost in a single incident which demonstrates incompetence or lack of integrity, or which could be interpreted as doing so and has been inadequately explained.

- Once lost, it is an extremely difficult and slow process to build up trust again.

What destroys trust is behaviour that is contradictory to the message you have been giving. In seeking an explanation for the discrepancy, especially when they feel hurt, people assume their leaders are incompetent or self-seeking. To avoid a loss of trust, then, you need to minimise the likelihood of surprises and apparent contradictions. This means educating people about likely future scenarios.

It seems that in the early twenty-first century we are particularly reluctant to trust our leaders. According to an Ipsos MORI poll in June 2007, 68 per cent of people believe that official figures are distorted to support leaders' arguments. In an earlier poll (June 2003) they discovered that 65 per cent of those in full-time employment did not believe that companies can be trusted to honour their pension commitments to employees.

The pre-target time is a good one to start building trust and to make sure that the infrastructure is in place to show trustworthiness throughout the process. Don't pretend to be what you're not.

There is usually some reluctance to communicate the wider strategic picture to employees:

- Executives may claim that this is because of Stock Exchange regulations about communicating price-sensitive information. You are not seeking to breach these regulations; you do not want or need to communicate more to employees than the finance director and CEO have already presented to analysts.

- It is usually possible to communicate more local financial information that relates to only part of the organisation, such as sales or profits in one branch or region. At worst it is always possible to give results compared with plan or budget. In most cases it is not the figures themselves that employees need but a sense of where the organisation is trying to get to and how well it is doing against that plan.

- There is a fear that senior managers will look foolish if the strategy fails or that it will be hard to communicate if the strategy changes. This reluctance is rooted in a fear that employees will not really understand the context behind the strategy and will not take the trouble to understand the reasons behind it. The answer is to keep communicating the wider context in which the organisation is operating, so that the rationale for changes can be understood.

Keeping people abreast with a changing strategy

One organisation had a strategy to build a great business in Asia with the aid of two partners. The strategy failed, partly because of changing priorities among the partners. It had to change its strategy completely, having put great effort into communicating the first strategy. It had to buy out the partners and find a different way of growing and making profits.

Although there was considerable fear in the company as it emerged that the Asian strategy was going to fail, the company was able to take people with them on the new strategy by continually communicating the options and their reasons for choosing the way forward they did.

- There will be concerns about communicating to the relevant employees if part of the organisation is to be sold off. The fear is that their morale will sink and that key people will leave, thus damaging performance and hence the price the organisation will sell for. This rationale is correct, providing there are no rumours. In practice, time after time we find that the top management think the matter is secret but in fact the rumours are everywhere, poisoning relations between the company and the part that is for sale.

The mistake of keeping quiet about divestment plans

In one organisation rumours were rife in one of the factories as people interpreted statements in the annual report and subsequently unexplained strangers were seen about the plant. The company would not answer questions about the site's future and insisted that it would be wrong to communicate as people would not feel valued if they realised that the company planned to sell the factory. The result of course was not just low morale throughout the time the organisation was trying to find a buyer, but a thoroughly difficult communication environment for the new owners, where the workforce did not trust any communication from any senior people.

Successful handling of outsourcing

In one outsourcing IT organisation they advise organisations to tell people as soon as possible what they are thinking of doing, in advance of taking over the IT Department. They even advise inviting them in to meet people before the tendering process is complete so that they can answer questions – even though they might not win the contract. They find it is quicker and easier for them to create good working relationships in the new organisation if people are not bitter or angry before the contract begins.

ENSURING THAT YOUR COMMUNICATION INFRASTRUCTURE IS UP-TO-DATE

Once an announcement is made you will be busy. You will need to rely on your basic infrastructure for communication. These are basic housekeeping points, but experience suggests that there are often problems here, which, unless they are put right, can trip you up or cause extra work when you are already overstretched later. You will need to be confident that you have:

- A way of reaching every employee individually. This may easily be available to you by email, but in most organisations, even now, there are some people who cannot or do not access email at work. These include, for example, catering staff, drivers, distribution and retail staff, and in some cases many more. Depending on the practicalities of your organisation you will either need a company or home address for each person, so that you can address them personally when an announcement is made.

- Organisation charts so that you know who reports to whom. Check that the method you use to keep organisation charts updated on your intranet actually works.

- A way of communicating with everyone extremely quickly. Depending on the nature of your workforce and the wealth of your company this may be by high-tech means such as satellite broadcast or by very low-tech means such as a fax arriving and being read out by the local manager. Make sure you have the various channels mapped out for all your sites, however small.

- Mobile phone numbers for all your senior managers so that they can be informed of developments quickly.

KEY PLAYERS

This work is likely to be led by the business development director if there is one. It may also be led by a strategy director. If not, it will probably be the CEO, typically working closely with the finance director. The strategy will have been agreed by the whole board of directors. Their aims will be strategic and the only communication considerations they are likely to have are external.

WHAT SORT OF LISTENING TO DO AT THIS STAGE

There is the ongoing and always necessary element of listening to understand the audience and its current views and knowledge. This means listening carefully to understand, so that you can enter a real dialogue, meeting concerns of different categories of employees and knowing what language to use that will have resonance with them.

It is also important to listen with a view to amending elements of the strategy in the light of knowledge or insights which emerge from listening to employees. This is of course a central dilemma of leadership: the need to have a constant vision for where the organisation is going and a strategy to take it there, while at the same time being open to new thinking and evidence. It is the thin line between determination and pig-headedness. It is the job of the leaders of the organisation to have a vision and to make a strategy to get there; it is, however, a mistake to ignore sensible objections to elements of the strategy or to be inflexible in the face of new evidence.

In some cases, the strategy itself can emerge following a listening exercise among senior people and those with high potential or in a good strategic position in the organisation. In one case where People in Business was involved, the Board invited us to conduct interviews with about 25 people in that category. They were clear that the organisation needed to make some bold acquisitions and expansions and their views influenced the board in setting an ambitious strategy, knowing that there was an appetite for it among the next tranche of management.

The major role for listening, however, is when the strategy is being implemented. Employees at every level have knowledge and experience which can improve plans for implementation, and we will return to this subject in Chapter 5: Stage Five.

The important principle in all consultation exercises is to be clear about what is still up for debate and amendment, and what has been decided. There is no point in wasting effort on decisions already taken.

It is axiomatic that we listen when we feel we are being listened to, and that when we feel no one is listening to us, we stop listening back. This is quite often the syndrome that affects communication about strategy. It is an essential part of the communicator's role to ensure that the leaders are able to engage in a real dialogue with employees and listen with a view to amendment, even if only in detail or emphasis. Your job is not just to fashion messages but to help create a relationship between the leaders and employees where trust grows and a real exchange of views results in better understanding by all parties.

In practical terms this listening can happen in various ways:

- with employee representatives in works councils or other consultative bodies;

- with employees attending special focus groups or meals with senior people;

- through regular employee surveys, particularly the "write in" parts;

- through feedback from team briefings, where the internal communication department receives notes on discussions and questions raised at meetings throughout the organisation;

- through the business planning process, if many people are involved in working out the detail of how the strategy is translated to budgets and other specific plans;

- through the ordinary sequence of management meetings;

- through particular change projects.

Good example of the sort of listening to do at Stage One

In Safeway, when the company was going through a period of culture change in the early 2000s, the Chief Executive ran regular focus groups with a cross-section of Head Office employees to hear first-hand how they were feeling and what their views were.

WHAT EMPLOYEES ARE THINKING AND SAYING

What You Want Employees to be Thinking and Saying

> This is an exciting organisation to be with. I want to build a career here.

> There are going to have to be changes as our firm merges or buys another. They won't necessarily be comfortable, but they are necessary.

What You Don't Want Employees to be Thinking and Saying

> I've heard a rumour we're being sold. Wouldn't surprise me. They haven't been investing in us recently. Why should we care about the company when it doesn't care about us?

> I'm expecting just to trudge along at this job until I retire.

> Don't make me laugh! That's the fifth strategy they've had in as many years and none of them actually make any difference.

> I'm fed up with change. Why can't our management just leave us alone and let us have some time to consolidate.

THE COST OF GETTING IT WRONG

Much of the cost of getting it wrong at this stage will not show until much later in the process. However, some symptoms of problems, caused or exacerbated by poor communication might be:

* Key senior people leaving the organisation as they disagree with the strategy or fear that there isn't one. (Of course, this may be a substantive disagreement and not merely a failure of communication).

* Poor communication or a silo mentality between people at the front end of the organisation. This is often a symptom of differing views

around the top table, where different directors have allowed or encouraged their teams to work in isolation from colleagues' teams.

- Poor morale in parts of the organisation where people have been able to guess that they are up for sale but have not been told. This may result in high absenteeism, poor quality, high turnover of staff and low productivity. This poor morale may extend to parts of the organisation you have no intention of selling but where rumours have started.

- High-potential people leaving if they cannot perceive a strategy and therefore cannot see a role for themselves in the future.

- Time being wasted gossiping about strategy and speculating about future moves.

SUMMARY FOR INTERNAL COMMUNICATORS

1. Really understand the organisation's context and strategy so that you are ready to explain it.

2. Make sure that the communication between members of the top team is as good as they think it is, and that they all actually mean the same thing when they use the same words.

3. Take steps to create a high level of understanding of that context and strategy among employees at all levels.

4. Ensure that your own infrastructure is robust and that you have the channels to communicate quickly and universally.

5. Make sure that employees are listened to and that there is space in decision-making to heed their views.

2 Stage Two: Due Diligence

In this chapter we look at the process whereby potential partners size each
other up in advance of making the final deal. Internal communication can
form a part of this process, especially looking at the cultural aspects of your
potential partner.

Due diligence typically has two main periods: before the approach to the
target (*covert*) and during negotiations (*overt*). There are of course millions of
variations on the theme of what is possible before and during negotiations,
depending on relationships between the parties. In the case of hostile bids,
it may not be possible to do much overt due diligence before buying a high
proportion of shares.

In some cases, therefore, the advice given in this chapter will be more relevant
after the deal has been made, or even after Day One when you have a chance
to investigate the target in more detail.

Research by Towers Perrin among HR executives (Schmidt 2002) demonstrates
clearly how much HR involvement in due diligence influences future
synergies. The research showed that 64 per cent of successful deals involved
HR in addressing cultural integration issues, compared with only 33 per cent
of unsuccessful deals.

COVERT DUE DILIGENCE

There is of course a covert element in even the most open of due diligence
processes: the bidder assesses both the individuals with whom they are
dealing as potential colleagues or negotiators and the culture of the
organisation they are looking at, even before they approach the target.

The detail of what is covered in the people aspects of due diligence varies
according to the reasons for the deal and the extent to which the bidder
would like to keep the current employees of the target. The more explicit the

bidder can be at this stage about what it is looking for and what it fears, the better both for the subsequent negotiations and for the eventual deal if one is made. If there is no plan to integrate then the cultural aspect of due diligence is much less relevant.

There are a number of ways of doing cultural- and communication-related due diligence. Alumni and existing staff are important sources of information. It may well be that you are already employing alumni of a potential target, who have brought with them knowledge of the target. Even if recruitment has been fruitless, the HR department or others involved in interviewing recent candidates from the target are likely to have good knowledge of what it was like as an employer.

If the target organisation is heterogeneous, and especially if it itself has been formed by a process of mergers and acquisitions rather than organic growth, it is important to understand the variety of cultures and practices within the organisation. There are also likely to be differences according to the various professional or craft groups. IT people, for example, tend to have their own particular culture, which is often quite distinct from that of the rest of the organisation.

Employment Agencies and other Recruiters

Employment agencies or graduate appointment bodies such as the career advice centres of major universities can also be useful sources of information. In this case it is easier to conduct the investigation simply by asking for information comparing one's own organisation with others, including the potential target in a list of other non-target organisations.

Checklist: Covert due diligence questions to ask employment agencies, headhunters and other recruiters

How would you compare us as an employer compared with various other organisations (of which the target is one)?

- attractiveness to top-class candidates of various categories, for example, technical, professional, managerial, graduates, and so on. and why or why not?

- ability to keep top-class talent of these sorts.

- ability to grow or develop people so that they deliver as well as they could.

- ability to motivate people.

Headhunters might also have an idea of the quality of the management of the target organisation at senior and even at middle levels.

Suppliers and Customers

Suppliers and customers can be approached in the same way, as it is not uncommon for organisations to want to benchmark themselves against others. The relevant questions to suppliers and customers might be something like the following.

Checklist: Covert due diligence questions to ask suppliers and customers on the subject of the culture of the target

How would you compare us as a customer or supplier with *[names of alternative organisations]* in terms of the people you deal with at all levels?

- reliability in meeting promises;

- speed of decision-making;

- ease of processes, for example, the people you deal with are not having to apologise for the lack of flexibility or speed of their processes;

- extent of empowerment/ability of front-line staff to deal with any problems themselves without having to refer upwards;

- competence of various types of staff;

- customer orientation/desire to help;

- knowledge, for example, of product, among staff of various sorts;

- flexibility.

If the target's profile is very different from your own then you know that integration will not be easy, and it may indicate which of the old organisations should lead in certain aspects of work in the new one.

Other Means of Covert Due Diligence

There is of course a mass of information in the public domain about organisations, and any good online library or information service can give access to press coverage going back over several years.

Looking more specifically at the people aspects, it is a matter of public record what awards the organisation may have won, for example, Investors in People or British Quality Foundation. Although a limited amount of detail may be publicly available, the very fact that the award has been given tells you something. In addition, there are numerous HR awards such as those given out by the various trade and professional publications and the Chartered Institute of Personnel Development (CIPD). On the communications front, there are Chartered Institute of Public Relations PRide awards in different categories, and the British Association of Communicators in Business awards. A number of the quality newspapers also run competitions for the best employers, including the *Sunday Times*, *The Guardian* and the *Financial Times*. Even though these competitions may miss great employers (who have not chosen to put themselves forward), organisations which get in the top 50 or 100 are unlikely to be poor employers; what is more, the case studies are usually written up in some detail in the relevant publications.

It is also worth searching for profiles of key executives in the relevant trade or professional press. For HR people this includes:

- *People Management.*

- *Human Resources.*

- *Personnel Today.*

And for communication people:

- *Strategic Communication Management.*

- The Institute of Public Relations and its publication *Profile.*

- THE CIB's publication *Communicate.*

An organisation's own website often provides information, sometimes revealing, about the sort of employer it attempts to be. Most company websites have recruitment or careers pages, and many have pages about their values or principles.

Some aspects of the target's employee relations record can also be examined. If the target recognises a union, go to the union's website and do a search for the organisation. It will tell you in some cases if there is an ongoing dispute with the organisation, although some sites are mainly closed to non-members. You can usually look at the union's press releases.

OVERT DUE DILIGENCE

As already mentioned, in some agreed mergers or acquisitions there may be a great deal of overt due diligence done before the deal is announced to the world at all, but sometimes the detailed due diligence is done between the announcement of the deal and finalisation.

However friendly the discussions, there will necessarily be some difficulties in the due diligence process. Inevitably the hosts will try to present the information they have in the best light, and the sheer volume of the data will mean that it is difficult for the bidders to take a completely objective view of it.

There are numerous checklists for due diligence, for example an excellent one produced by Roffey Park. It is not the purpose of this book to go into the detail of most of it. Suffice it to say that due diligence should cover not just the figures but every aspect of relationships with key stakeholders and the processes inside the organisation. The communicator needs to work most closely with HR colleagues, as the communication work is closely aligned to HR's work, partly because both concern culture and the psychological contract, and partly because people issues are central to communication.

There will be other areas where your HR colleagues will be concentrating their attention, and it may be that your areas of interest are so closely aligned that the processes should be run together. In particular they will be looking at:

- identification of key talent, both at management and at specialist level;

- which aspects of terms and conditions are most valued by employees, and how expensive they might be to keep or to change;

- buried "booby traps" such as agreements giving generous relocation packages, redundancy terms, and so on, which may make integration expensive.

There are two areas of due diligence where you will be particularly involved:

1. cultural due diligence;

2. communication due diligence.

Cultural Due Diligence

Study after study of merger waves has shown that two of every three deals have not worked...look behind any disastrous deal and the same word keeps popping up – culture. Culture permeates a company and differences can poison any collaboration.

The Economist, January 1999

There are numerous classification systems and taxonomies for measuring culture. According to Edgar Schein (1996) there are three layers of culture:

1. explicit products, for example language, buildings, fashions, artefacts;

2. norms and values;

3. implicit assumptions (to test if something is a basic assumption see if questioning it causes confusion or provokes irritation).

There are, of course, several dimensions of culture: people reflect their own national or regional culture, that of their profession or craft, their generation and social class, as well as the culture within their particular organisation. Even within one professional group in one organisation there may be very different cultures reflecting previous ownership or management. Assessing culture is therefore not easy, since people draw on different aspects of their background when faced with different challenges.

Although, as we have seen, it is possible to do some covert cultural due diligence, once the proposed deal is public it is possible to do it more overtly. It is vital to conduct some sort of cultural analysis of both parties to the deal, not just to look at the target. There are probably assumptions you are making about the bidder organisation and it is important to subject both cultures to the same rigorous assessment.

Definition:

Culture: The way in which a group of people solve problems and reconcile dilemmas (Trompenaars).

An early exercise is to try to list the important different subcultures that are likely to exist in each company. These are likely to reflect:

- discipline: different professional and craft groups are likely to have their own cultures and ways of doing things;

- history;

- previous ownership;

- previous management;

- geography: both across national boundaries and within the UK.

There are over 25 off-the-shelf questionnaire-style assessments of culture for due diligence purposes, usually based on various academic theories. Choosing the appropriate one for you is likely to depend on a number of different factors:

- existing use of one of these models in one or other of the organisations meaning that there is already some data and you do not need to start from scratch in both organisations;

- the aspirations for the new organisation which may indicate a certain framework for looking at culture;

- whether or not the proposed deal is cross-border, in which case some of the international models are likely to be more useful.

Where does power lie?

One of the aspects of culture which you will need to explore is discovering where power really lies in the organisation, as opposed to the apparent structure from an organisation chart. Where the real power lies may be a function of the following:

- Personal relationships, as some managers have particularly strong characters or strong alliances with others.

- A professional function or department, which may have historical reasons relating to individuals but which now may be deeply rooted and is manifested in such things as who can veto decisions, who needs to be consulted before they are taken (the power of finance and HR departments, for example, varies greatly).

- Customer or owner-focus. In whose interests are decisions taken? Sales or customer-service people who remain close to customers? Or finance or operations people who are often looking more carefully at costs or thinking about how to impress analysts.

- It is worth finding out where the turf wars take place between departments and which ones tend to ally with each other.

- The personal interests and experience of the chief executive tend to influence where power lies.

Other dimensions of culture

There may be other evident differences in organisations, which can impede their integration. These include:

- Attitudes towards diversity: to what extent is the organisation dominated by one type of person, typically white male?

- Attitudes towards external stakeholders: including the extent to which corporate social responsibility is taken seriously. It is worth being aware of which features of the organisation are valued by its various stakeholders.

Management

It can be useful to conduct a series of one-to-one interviews with managers as part of cultural due diligence. This is not the same as any assessment programme for their suitability for the new organisation (although there may be some overlap), but a means of understanding the culture in the new organisation and seeing how different it is from that within your own.

Depending on relationships, and in some cases on regulatory requirements, you may not be able to access the new management until after the deal is finalised. Table 2.1 shows some useful questions to ask, if you can. If you can't access the new management during due diligence, then these are questions to ask as quickly as possible after it.

Table 2.1   Questions to ask new management during due diligence

What you ask	How to interpret it
Extent to which they feel engaged with the stated strategy of the organisation.	There is some good news if they are not truly engaged. It implies that managers will not be so wedded to the old organisation's strategy that they will find it hard to change allegiance to the new one. On the other hand, there is bad news too. It may imply that managers have not been much developed or educated in wider strategic thinking, a gap which the new organisation will have to fill.
Extent to which different managers have the same view of the strategy.	If there is a consistent view it is likely to mean that communication has been good in the target organisation. On the other hand, if there is no disagreement, and no different vocabulary being used, then it would imply a worrying lack of challenge and thought by anyone except the most senior person or team. Ideally there should be unanimity on understanding the current strategy and the reasons for it, but one would also expect some individual viewpoints, showing that there was depth in management taking a responsibility for thinking about the future and issues facing the organisation. You would also be looking to see the extent to which there was silo thinking, with people giving responses that narrowly relate to their area of the business only, or the extent to which managers were taking an interest in the wider organisation. If managers have been accustomed to silo thinking this may be a problem if you plan to integrate the new organization.
How big are the differences in vocabulary and attitude between the most senior managers and less senior and middle managers?	A big difference implies a lack of investment in education or communication with more junior managers.

Table 2.1 *Concluded*

Their knowledge of the competition and broad context in which the organisation is operating, including the relevant political, social, economic and technological issues likely to impact on it.	Again, a big difference implies a lack of investment in education or communication with more junior managers.
What they think the reasons for the success of the organisation to date have been?	Listen for how much they concentrate only on their part of the organisation and how sophisticated their analysis is. How aware are they of competitors? Of global as opposed to local factors impacting on the organisation? Of political and social impact?
What they think are the main things the organisation needs to get right in the next few years?	Listen both for sophistication and for unanimity.
What are they most proud of and what are they most ashamed of in the organisation?	This is useful at face value.
Who do they regard as the heroes of the organisation and why?	Are they rebels or high achievers? It tells you a lot about the culture to hear the sort of activities or characteristics which have earned them hero status.
Give examples of actual decision-making.	Which departments are involved? To what extent are managers empowered to make their own decisions? To what extent are front-line employees, or those who will have to implement the decision, involved?
Give an example of something that has gone wrong in the organisation. What happened and has anything changed as a result?	Interesting to see how open they are. If they choose an example which was clearly not much of a howler at all it *may* mean that the organisation has never committed any howlers. More likely it means that the interviewee is nervous of sharing mistakes, and this may imply a reluctance to talk about or learn from bad news in the organisation, especially if nothing has changed as a result of the mistake.

Language

Looking at language has two useful functions: first it is useful to assess to what extent there is a common language throughout the organisation. Second, language reveals much about conceptual systems, as Table 2.2 shows.

Table 2.2   Due diligence: what language can tell you

What to look for	Implications
Is there a common language throughout the organisation? Or are different terms used for the same thing in different parts, or the same terms used to mean different things?	If there is a common language it might mean that there is a strong internal culture, which will make it harder to change the culture. However, it also means that there is likely to be a reasonable internal communication infrastructure. If there are different languages, it is worth noting where they are different. If, for example, customer facing staff have a different vocabulary or meaning of their words than other staff, it might imply that the rest of the organisation had little understanding of customer needs. If there is a difference between the language used by management and that used by other employees it might imply that communication between the two has been poor. If the language used by specialists doing the same sort of work around the organisation is different it would imply that there has been little sharing of practice or learning around the company.
Clues to conceptual frameworks about colleagues.	It is particularly revealing if any derogatory or minimising words are used in parts of the organisation. Witty soubriquets about Head Office, for example, will have caught on if they reflect a resentment of Head Office power in the branches. Departments or functions with nicknames are also likely to have resented power. ("Human Remains Department", "Inhuman Resources" and so on)
Clues to conceptual frameworks about customers.	If the organisation's customers are referred to without respect, for example by the use of the word "punter" or worse, this reveals a particular attitude to customer relations.
Clues to conceptual frameworks about suppliers and other partners.	Again a lack of respect in language and tone may imply potential difficulties in working across the new organisation. It is also likely to mean that, in practice, relationships may not be as strong as the contracts may imply.
Clues to power distance.	If people are referred to throughout by their first names rather than titles or initials it implies lower power distance.

Artefacts
You can tell a lot about the culture of the place simply by walking around.

Table 2.3   Due diligence: what artefacts can tell you

Where to look	What to look for	Implications
Reception – staff.	Engaged and efficient reception staff: are they expecting you? Do they know immediately how to reach the person you are seeing or do they have to ask each other or a third party?	If the service is not efficient it implies a lack of attention to administration and may also imply a lack of interest in customers.
Reception – the look and feel.	How much does it reflect the image the organisation tries to project elsewhere? If the organisation portrays itself as technological and modern, is this reflected in the displays and décor in Reception, or does the area seem to be a left-over from a previous regime? Is company material such as corporate brochures and marketing materials up-to-date?	Again, this shows the amount of emphasis placed on customers. Also, whether the organisation has pride in itself, a feature which is an important element in a successful employer brand.
The person who comes to get you.	Is it the person you have come to see?	If so, it implies either that the visit is being kept extremely secret or that the organisation is quite egalitarian and senior people do not automatically send their secretaries.
	If it is a PA or junior, does he/she introduce themselves?	To do so implies a level of confidence in dealing with outsiders and newcomers, which augurs well for future work across the organisations.
The look and feel of the offices.	Like Reception, the issue here is not just the expensiveness or modernity of the desks and equipment but their consistency with the external message.	

Table 2.3   *Continued*

Layout of office.	Open plan, cubicle or offices: each has implications for how people tend to relate to each other.	The more open the office the more open the day-to-day communication is likely to be.
Office décor.	Do the desks give the impression that the people working there are interested in their work? Are the notices or papers on the wall related to the work and performance or are they entirely related to home and outside-work activities or interests?	If they are all related to outside-work interests that would indicate a lack of engagement in the work of the organisation. On the other hand, if there are no pictures of family or friends it would imply a workplace where people do not feel able to bring their whole selves to work.
Offices of senior executives.	In the target is there a bigger difference in working environment according to status, for example, in office furniture ?	If so, managers in the target organisation might be nervous of losing status in the new organisation.
	Secretaries' desks guard the senior executives from the rest of the organisation	A hierarchical organisation where people of all levels do not drop in to talk and where probably the senior people are isolated and ignorant about the thoughts and feelings of more junior staff.
	Are they together or are they dotted around to be with their departments?	If together they are likely to be more cohesive, but there is a danger that they will be insulated from feelings elsewhere in the organisation.
Directors' suite (if it exists).	How different is the standard of furnishing and decoration?	If there is a major mismatch with yours then it implies there are likely to be cultural differences between the new top teams.
Common and dining areas.	Are there separate dining facilities for different grades of staff, and if so, how different are the different facilities? Also, how much money has been spent on staff areas?	What does this indicate about how valued staff are? How different is it from your own offices?

Table 2.3   *Concluded*

Behaviour of colleagues as you walk through offices.	Do people look up and smile or do they bury themselves in their work? As you pass, what sort of conversations can you hear people have, and with whom? If they are talking on the phone, what is their tone of voice? Are they talking to customers or suppliers or are the calls internal? Are they personal calls? Are colleagues talking to each other? If so, do they appear to be engaged in dynamic discussions where people are raising alternative points of view or are they merely checking things with each other or, worse still, talking about non-work subjects altogether?	The sort of ratio to expect will naturally vary according to the work being done in the office, but too many external conversations might indicate a silo mentality, whereas too many internal would indicate a bureaucracy that was keeping people away from the important external contacts. Lack of lively discussion may indicate a lack of innovation and an avoidance of conflict. There may be some complaisance.
Noticeboards.	Are they busy or clear? What is the balance between personal or social and work content? Are the boards well signposted? Are the union boards better and more prominent than the company ones?	There should be a good distinction between company, social and union boards. If the union board dominates it implies that the union, rather than the company, is leading in communication. A preponderance of kittens for sale, caravans to let, and so on, implies that people are insufficiently engaged in their work, but a complete absence of it implies that people are not creating strong relationships at work.
Dress code.	How similar to that in the bidder?	If very different from the bidder's, it may create difficulties later on.

As well as one-to-one interviews with managers it can be useful to talk to other staff at the due diligence stage. If it is not possible to organise special focus groups, it may be possible to ask questions of employees gathered together for other purposes such as consultative groups or training courses. You should ask a similar set of questions as those asked of managers, adding a question about what sort of people thrive in the organisation; this is a useful cultural question showing what is really valued in the organisation.

It is also worth asking about any explicit culture programmes that the organisation has done, for example on customer relations, living the brand or values programmes. Their ultimate impact, of course, can be detected from the cultural measures we have indicated, but having had unsuccessful programmes can actually make it harder for a subsequent programme to succeed if it has bred cynicism and raised expectations it has failed to meet.

Readiness for Change

Another aspect of culture is readiness for change. Generally, the more change people have already undergone, the more ready they will be for it, and the more confident they will be that they can cope with it.

Whatever the integration strategy for the new organisation, a merger or acquisition is likely to imply some change for people in the new organisation. Our experience is that ability to change is a competence learned by experience; individuals and organisations develop confidence in change by practice. Knowing how ready the target is for change is therefore useful. In some cases there may be a suspicion that it was failure to change or adapt quickly enough that has led the organisation to becoming a target in the first place; in these instances in particular it is important to find out if the failure to change was the result of managerial lack of foresight or a deeper cultural phenomenon.

Checklist: Change readiness

Below are some indicators of experience of change. The more ticks you have on this checklist the more likely the target is to be able to change readily.

A high proportion of people have within the past two years:

* implemented or been involved with the implementation of a major technology change;

* been reorganised in such a way that the actual working teams have changed (that is, more than changing the offices and job titles of senior people);

* have relocated;

* have had a complete overhaul of jobs including grading, titles and so on.

- have had a major training intervention.

Danger signs would be:

- Evidence of industrial action or the threat of industrial action over proposed change.

- Abandoned culture change initiatives: not only are these a sign that the employees proved obdurate in the face of cultural change but the very fact of the failure may have strengthened the forces of resistance. It is worth looking carefully at the proposed changes and the reasons for abandonment, however. It may be that the residual benefits of the programme outweigh the resistance or cynicism the failure has engendered. Our experience is that the first culture change initiative in an organisation rarely succeeds, however well planned and executed. The organisation's powers of rejection almost inevitably see it off. However, there are usually some residual practices and some subtly changed attitudes from the exercise which make subsequent change programmes more likely to succeed.

Previous Associations

It is worth looking specifically at any previous attempts to work with other organisations. This will obviously include any previous mergers or acquisitions but could also cover joint ventures, contracting out or partnership arrangements of one sort or another, where employees have had to work alongside people in another organisation.

Questions to ask about previous associations

1. How well did relationships work?

2. What means were developed for dealing with difficulties or disagreements? Did they work?

3. What formal means of joint planning or working together were developed? How many people were involved in them?

4. In what sort of terms did people not directly involved with the partner organisation speak of it?

You are looking for two sorts of activity here:

1. the sort of attitudes that people will consciously or unconsciously carry forward to the new deal;

2. specific expertise in working with people outside the confines of the organisation itself.

Communication Due Diligence

Understanding the networks in the two organisations

Alongside the formal organisation chart and processes, informal networks tell people what is going on inside and outside the organisation, and conduct much of the day-to-day business. Before tampering with the organisation it is useful to know how it actually works at present. This will both help with the immediate communication of the merger and inform the workstreams so that they do not unwittingly destroy the networks which make either organisation successful.

How to trace networks

It is hard to trace networks systematically. The most usual way is by asking people to complete some sort of diary, noting who they speak to in person and on the phone and who they email over a period of time. Alternatively, specialised questionnaires can be used, asking people who they talk to on certain sorts of topics. Either way the results can then be mapped, showing who are the key "nodes" (see Figure 2.1).

In practice this demands more work than you are often able to devote to it at this stage in the merger. A version can, however, be pulled together in a workshop or team meeting which would at least give guidance about how people actually receive information and who is likely to be influencing whom. This would be useful to know in both organisations.

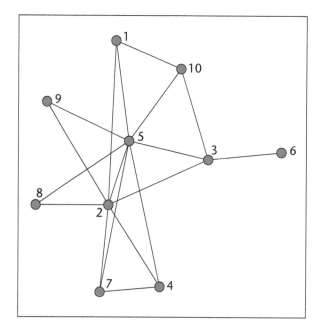

Figure 2.1   Example of a social network diagram

Source: Hanneman and Riddle 2005.

How to assess communication in the two organisations

There are two different reasons for looking at the communication frameworks in both organisations: the first is that frameworks both reflect and lead organisational culture, so that studying the communication will tell you about working relationships and ability to change; the second is that you are going to need to use both systems in the run up to Day One and indeed on Day One itself, and, in all probability, for at least the beginning of the first 100 days. If the systems are completely different, you will need to be running two communication strategies until such time as you have been able to merge the functions; if they are similar, you may be able to work with one strategy with slightly different manifestations to take advantage of the local facilities. Dimensions to look for:

- credibility;
- mixture of local and senior sources;
- ability to ask questions;
- ability to put up suggestions;
- involvement in innovation and problem solving;
- lateral communication;
- degree of big picture compared with local messages;
- extent of education/communication on business context as well as inside view;
- clarity and relevance of performance information at various levels;
- clarity of leadership voice;
- ability to communicate quickly.

Table 2.4   Due diligence: assessing communication in the two organisations

What to look for	Implications if it is good	Implications if it is bad
Credibility as revealed by: Employee survey results. Tone of comments on intranet or other upward channels. Union or other employee representatives' views.	Old organisation sources can be used for immediate announcements.	Will have an uphill struggle with communication from the start. Will need to be careful to make sure anything you say will happen when you said it would. Be wary of making too many promises or optimistic generalisations.

Table 2.4   *Continued*

What to look for	Implications if it is good	Implications if it is bad
Mixture of local and senior sources: People are used to receiving some information directly from senior people.	If there is too much identification with one leader, it can make subsequent communication difficult, especially if the leader does not stay with the organisation or is ambiguous about the deal.	You will have to do a great deal of work with senior managers as they will be perceived as the only credible source. If there is likely to be a high turnover in the senior management in the target this may pose problems later.
People are used to receiving information from their line managers.	You will need to do a great deal of work with the line managers as there is a danger that they will be threatened by the deal and not be positive about it. Also, people will expect to receive answers to their local questions and may find it hard to live with uncertainty.	There is probably a degree of cynicism about company announcements if they are not being reinforced by local management. There are probably other face-to-face sources which carry credibility; you need to find out what they are and try to influence them.
There are facilities for asking questions and getting responses, either by intranet, telephone services or other means.	These will be extremely useful to you. If this is better in the target than in the bidder there will need to be some quick work bringing the bidder up to speed.	Again, if there is no proper source, there are likely to be informal and possibly ill-informed ones. Beware of setting unrealistic expectations if you attempt to set up a system for answering questions, as it is unlikely that you will have answers for some time.
There are facilities for putting up suggestions.	Need to keep them going as business as usual, as well as encouraging ideas emerging from Day One.	Will make little difference to the communication of Day One.
Involvement in innovation and problem-solving.	People will expect to be involved in workstreams.	There may be a reluctance to get involved and a tendency to wait and see and then criticise.

Table 2.4 *Concluded*

Good lateral communication with communities of practice or other informal cross-fertilisation of ideas across the organisation.	Need to be aware of the timing of announcements as these networks will spread interesting information fast.	This may be an area where the deal can add substantial value if communities of practice can be set up across the new organisation.
There is good communication of big picture information as well as local.	People will have some expectation of the business case being communicated to them and probably some level of education on business terms and concepts.	People may have difficulty understanding the big picture and will be less impressed by business arguments. They are likely only to want to know about local implications.
There is good communication about the industry and economy context in which the organisation works, for example knowledge of competitors and their strategies.	People here may well have anticipated a deal of some sort and will be less surprised. They will expect and be ready to hear the sort of information the City and trade publications will be receiving.	See above. There will be little thirst for anything except immediate information about local matters. There may well be some ill-informed rumours.
There is good and regular performance information at team and other local levels.	People will be able to keep their eye on business as usual during the time of uncertainty.	People are likely to be distracted by rumours and may have unrealistically optimistic views of their performance compared with others'.
There is a clear leadership voice in the organisation, rather than different senior managers at different levels each having active communication with all employees.	Providing the voice is clear and positive about the deal and reinforces the reasons for it, the communication will be clearer for people.	There is likely to some cynicism anyway among employees where there are too many leadership voices vying for attention.
There is an ability to communicate quickly to everyone, for example, by email.	This will be extremely useful when there are announcements. If the target is ahead of the bidder it is worth thinking about bringing the bidder up to speed as quickly as possible.	Lack of this channel will seriously hamper communication. If possible, find a way of communicating quickly with everyone, even if it has to be low tech.

Lateral communication and knowledge sharing

The need for knowledge sharing will of course vary according to the nature of the organisation and its workforce. Having structures and practices for knowledge sharing is particularly important when:

- similar work is done by people working in separate teams, perhaps because of geographical dispersion (for example, Xerox did a great deal of work in the late 1990s with photocopier service engineers based all over the world facing the same issues and needing to communicate with each other);

- there is a traditional rather than a matrix structure and/or when there is not a strong disciplinary tradition where rules from Head Office govern every part of the work;

- technology is advancing quickly, offering the opportunity for beating competitors to the market if advances by some individuals and teams can be shared across all of them;

- labour turnover is high and there is a danger that expertise will be lost with the people who leave.

It is also worth checking anyway how well documented processes are. It is likely that key people will leave following the deal, whether at your behest or theirs, and it is important to make sure that you can continue to conduct the business without them.

The dangers of failing to map knowledge

Quote from a focus group attendee in a recently merged organisation where knowledge had not been mapped: "The network diagram for the system is in Matthew's head and he's leaving today."

Employee survey data

It is of course useful to know how engaged people are, how high their morale is and whether their attachment is to their work, their immediate colleagues or to the organisation, or indeed if there is little attachment at all. One of the things the bidder is buying is the expertise, knowledge and reputation of the workforce. Research indicates that 75 per cent of senior managers leave acquired companies within five years, and 60 per cent of all managers leave within five years (Walsh 1988). Obviously some of these exits are not regretted by the acquirer, but some are. In one organisation, for example, due diligence failed to discover very low morale among a salesforce. When many of them left as soon after the acquisition as they could, the business was badly harmed. Any hints that many or key people are likely to leave following the deal should be taken into account in negotiations.

Employee survey data is obviously a rich source for you, as well as for your HR colleagues. There are various points to look for specifically, if the data is available:

- Response rates: if the response rates are low (below 60 per cent) not only is the data fairly suspect but it indicates a degree of disengagement by employees that they have not bothered to complete the form. Either they have given up hope that things will improve or they have no faith in the confidentiality of the survey. Either way it indicates low trust.

- Comparative results among different populations: it is useful to cut the data by site, level and occupational group at least, to see if there are any particular groups which appear to have been left behind.

- Look carefully at the results for the middle managers: they should have good scores on questions about believing the organisation knows where it's going and feeling well informed about strategy. Look for questions indicating emotional involvement such as pride in the organisation, recommending it to others, and so on. In particular check that their scores are at least as good as those of the rest of the organisation. People will look to these middle managers as change happens in the new organisation. Obviously there is work to do once the deal has happened to bring them alongside, but it helps if they were already engaged in their former organisation.

- Questions about emotional engagement are important for all audiences as this will give you an idea of how likely they are to want a new organisation to succeed. However, if emotional engagement is very high it might also imply some difficulty if the proposed deal might involve losing the very elements that people feel pride in.

- Read *all* the verbatim comments that people have written in open questions, or at least choose them at random. Do not look only at those chosen to go in the final report. The tone and language used in the verbatims is a useful first-hand indicator of how people feel about the organisation. Also, see how many of them refer to the business and suggestions for improving it compared with suggestions about pay or other transactional issues. This can give an indication of how much people care about the business as well as their personal well-being.

- Look at any questions relating to credibility and trust. We have already noted the importance of trust. If there is cynicism about what various sources or individuals say, you need to be aware of this, not just for planning purposes, but because it will make it harder for the new organisation to establish credible channels if people do not trust the ones they have.

Beware of imagining that the same issues underlie similar scores, either within an organisation or across them. Similar climate issues (for example, job satisfaction or the extent to which people feel informed about performance) can have similar scores but mask significant differences in expectation and actual practice.

Other sources of employee insight

In addition to the formal employee survey, there are likely to be other sources, which may or may not be available as part of due diligence. They include:

- Information from termination interviews – if it is collated. Though people are not always honest, even when they know they are leaving an organisation, emerging patterns can be revealing. If people claim always to be leaving solely for the money – when you know pay rates are competitive – that may imply that they do not feel they can be honest even in a termination interview. If not it would be useful to see if their complaints were about individual managers, their own chances for advancement or their perceptions of the culture of the organisation itself. The sort of insight that can be particularly valuable at this stage might be about what sort of people are perceived to succeed in the organisation.

- Information from appraisal interviews or personal development plans – again, if it is collated. It would be useful to see to what extent issues raised reflect an understanding of the future strategy of the business or to what extent they are largely transactional, for instance looking for more money or more convenient hours.

- Chat rooms or question areas on the intranet. The tone of these is frequently negative, and that in itself does not tell you much about the organisation. But it can be useful to see how negative the tone is, and what sorts of characteristics are imputed to the organisation. Are managers in the organisation portrayed as foolish or incompetent, or as trying to pull a fast one on employees? (Useful to know later on when looking to communicate.) Do some people defend management or is the tone uniformly negative?

- Questions asked in team briefings or at company conferences, and so on. Look for the extent of knowledge or ignorance the questions imply. Look also for how broad people's perceptions are. Do they ask only about very local issues? To what extent do they appear to be close to customers by the nature of the questions they ask?

- Minutes of the employee council or consultative committees. In particular look for issues going on for meeting after meeting without being resolved. This implies that the council is not really achieving much. Look for statements where one side compliments the other or thanks them for their help.

- Minutes of union–management meetings. As above. Also, look to see if the union is concerned only with the pay-and-benefits sort of topic or whether it also interested in the success of the enterprise. To what extent does it talk about training and development for its members? The broader the agenda, the easier it will later be to work with the union in partnership.

Hard figures to look at

- Labour turnover. Generally speaking a high turnover will indicate dissatisfaction, but there may be other considerations.

- Number of formal grievances raised. If none, it may imply that people are frightened to raise grievances. (As one interviewee expressed it: "You'd have to have a death wish to go over the head of the Departmental Manager here".) If lots, it might imply real frustration and even desperation. It would also imply that informal channels were not relied on.

- Number of disciplinary proceedings and how many go to dismissal. Again, none might imply lax management rather than superb recruitment. On the other hand, many would imply poor recruitment and probably poor management that the organisation was failing to turn around mediocre performers.

- Number of employment tribunal cases, and what proportion won, lost or settled (and on what sort of terms). Any organisation can have tribunal claims, but losing tribunals (or settling to avoid imminent defeat) implies poor HR practices or more likely managers failing to seek support from HR, which itself might indicate a weak HR presence.

- Absence levels. Again, look at industry comparators as absence rates vary according to the nature of the work. A high absence rate implies low morale and/or weak performance management.

- Proportion of promotions internally filled. Too many and there might be a dangerous lack of new thinking; too few and it implies low calibre of existing staff and/or insufficient development of them. If the senior levels of the organisation are all or almost all recent recruits, they may be less able than long-serving people to keep their finger on the pulse of how people in the organisation are thinking. If the organisation has not felt able to promote its own people, it augurs ill for you finding many future managers for the combined organisation there.

- Proportion of people involved in working parties or consultative arrangements of one sort or another. The more people involved, the more likely they are to have problem-solving skills and project-working experience which may be useful after the deal.

DUE DILIGENCE ON TRADE UNION RELATIONS

This of course is a key area for your HR colleagues. They will be looking at the recognition agreements and seeing what hidden time-bombs there may be in agreements already entered into, and assessing how expensive it might be to buy out a myriad of varying terms and conditions. This is not so relevant for you, but the relationship with the union and its lay and full-time officials *is* of prime importance for you. One of the roles of unions is to inform its members about matters relevant to them. They are sure to have a line on the merger, and it is important for you that it is a positive one. At this stage you may be able to meet with and talk to union representatives at all levels. This is useful not just for what they tell you but also in sending them a message about your willingness to listen, which will be useful in the new organisation. Talk to full-time officials as well as the senior lay representatives in the organisation. Depending on the size of the organisation and the nature of its representation, this may be local, sector or general secretary level.

Questions to ask Union Officials

1.	See Table 2.5. You will want to get information about these matters and see how their views match those of the employer.

2.	How well informed do they think members are about the issues facing the organisation, competitive pressures, impact of change or regulations, and so on? This is a useful question not just for the answer but because it will enable you to gauge their own levels of awareness.

3.	How ready do they think people are for change? What will help and hinder their acceptance of it?

We will talk further in Chapter 3 about communication with the union regarding the proposed deal. At this stage the object is simply to assess the likelihood of developing or maintaining positive relationships in the new organisation.

**Table 2.5	Due diligence: communication with unions**

What to look for	Implications
1. Meetings: level	
Meetings at various levels, from national or international to local site or even departmental level.	Likely to be a large number of people involved in union affairs with, potentially, a good knowledge of the company (see content below).
Meetings on a regular basis at local levels but not at national or international level.	There may well be strong local loyalties to particular sites, which may itself cause problems if there is a plan to rationalise sites.

Table 2.5   *Concluded*

Meetings at national or international level only.	You may well find that there is a small kernel of union people, probably full-time officials, with good understanding of the issues, but this may well not be reflected among the rank-and-file members and representatives, who could cause trouble later.
2. Meetings: content	
Negotiations only.	Unlikely to be much sympathy or understanding for the company. Likely to hear any statement as an initial bargaining position.
Meetings include serious presentations on the context and issues facing the company. (This may include other employee representatives in a works council or similar.)	Likely to be a much better educated union group.
Meetings on larger issues allow plenty of time for discussion and even joint problem solving.	Better still. Union officials are likely to have a deeper understanding of the issues and some sympathy with the challenges faced by the organisation.
3. Relationships	
Only at a local level with lay and local full-time officials.	Good relationships at any level are worth having. This is likely to make change easier.
Relationships at a senior level, with either party able to lift the phone at any time and talk through problems.	A real strength. Where there is change it is helpful to be able to talk through the potential difficulties in advance and have the mechanisms and relationship to make a deal which all parties feel is fair.
4. Communication	
Tone of union communication to members is measured and accurate.	A good sign.
Tone of communication is angry and indignant.	This is a bad sign. Not only does it indicate that relationships are poor but it is likely to reflect the views of at least some of the readership, your future employees.
Union publications are well circulated and read.	This sets at least a minimum standard for you to match with company information in the new organisation.

ESTABLISHING RELATIONSHIPS WITH YOUR OPPOSITE NUMBERS DURING DUE DILIGENCE

Regulatory limitations may prevent you from meeting and talking with your opposite numbers. However, the way you conduct yourself during due diligence sends out strong messages and your (and the organisation's) reputation will go before you. It is part of your role to ensure that people engaged in due diligence are aware of this. Simple good manners are free. Unfortunately, the fact that you are negotiating makes it natural to stress the negative findings as you go through the process. Targets often feel bruised by comments made during negotiations and these bad feelings can spill over into their feelings about the bidder. In Chapter 3 we will look in more detail at establishing a relationship with your opposite number.

POTENTIAL DIFFICULTIES WITH DUE DILIGENCE

Much of this may be academic at the time of negotiations if either the target or regulatory bodies prevent exchange of information. If this is the case, the principles still apply to exchange of information later in the process.

POTENTIAL IMPACT ON THE ORGANISATION OF KEY PEOPLE LEAVING

As it is likely that people will leave following the merger, it is worth considering how great the impact of this will be on the business. The following are some key questions to ask:

- To what extent are key customers "owned" by individual sales people or account managers? Will you keep the business if the person goes?

- The same goes for key supplier relationships. Are they dependent on long-standing personal relationships?

- What is the engine room of the business, where the value is created? How easy would it be to maintain quality and productivity if many of the current job-holders left?

KEY PLAYERS

At this stage the main players are likely to be the same as at Stage One: senior business development personnel, finance and line management. You can get involved and undertake the exercises proposed in this chapter if a wider team engages in due diligence, covering human as well as business factors.

WHAT SORT OF LISTENING TO DO AT THIS STAGE

Since you are not actually communicating out at this stage, all your work is listening.

WHAT EMPLOYEES ARE THINKING AND SAYING

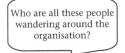

Who are all these people wandering around the organisation?

Are the rumours true?

THE COST OF GETTING IT WRONG

The communicator's role in due diligence is different from other times, in that your focus is on investigation rather than engaging with the rest of the organisation publicly. The egg-on-face potential is therefore not so immediate, but it is at least as important as the more public parts of your job. Drawing attention to potential communication and cultural hurdles could swing the decision-makers against a deal altogether, if it was deemed that the cost of overcoming the difficulties was going to be too great. Alternatively, if you fail to point out problems, or are too diffident in pressing their importance, and the deal goes ahead without price adjustment, much value may subsequently be lost.

The other potential cost of getting it wrong relates to the next stage of preparing the announcement. If you have failed to read the culture or correctly assess the communication capabilities, the chances of your managing the announcement or the communication of the first 100 days well are slim. You may also succeed in antagonising your opposite numbers during the process.

SUMMARY FOR INTERNAL COMMUNICATORS

1. Work done during due diligence to assess the culture and communication capacity of the potential partner can be useful both in influencing negotiations and in ensuring success should the deal go ahead.

2. You will need to work particularly closely with your HR colleagues at this stage.

3. It will also be useful to make sure that you know what your own communication infrastructure is and be confident that important messages can be communicated quickly, including face-to-face as far as possible.

3 Stage Three: The Initial Announcement

With planning the initial announcement we at last come to a time when your skills are bound to be valued. In the earlier stages you will probably have had little to do with the choice of a potential partner and, although you have an important job when a specific partner is in sight and there is a need to assess their suitability, you may have had a comparatively small role in due diligence. Finally, when it comes to the announcement everyone will acknowledge your importance.

The amount of detail that you are able to announce varies enormously. In cases where the merger is a friendly one, as for example with Norwich Union and CGU, some of the key decisions about the composition of the top team, the name of the new organisation and even some decisions such as the location of its Head Office may have been made before any public announcement. In other cases, especially if the approach is hostile, or if the announcement is in response to a leak, there is much less to say at this time. If the communication is in response to a leak or speculation there may not even be a deal to announce, but merely a holding statement about talks taking place.

At this stage you will need to be working with the other communication professionals in the organisation to make sure that the message is absolutely clear and consistent across the audiences, but that the framing for employees is appropriate for them and their concerns. You will also need to be working with line management or your local communications network to ensure that the communication of the announcement reflects a professionalism which will set the tone for the rest of the communication throughout the period before Day One and integration.

In this chapter we first consider the timetable and process leading up to the announcement, including the necessity for contingency planning in case of leaks. We then move on to the practical issues involved in preparing the announcements, the logistics of communication within both organisations, the content of an announcement pack and the particular issues of communicating with unions.

TIMETABLE OF A DEAL

The practice varies according to how friendly the arrangement is. The following are the stages likely in a hostile or competitive bidding situation. Some of these steps may be done invisibly or skipped altogether if the managements of the two sides agree among themselves.

> *Step 1*: Bidder may start buying up shares. Once they have 3 per cent they have to declare their shareholding publicly. This does not necessarily mean they are a bidder; institutional and other shareholders often hold 3 per cent or more of an organisation's stock without any intention of buying the whole company. In a friendly bid there may be no buying of shares at this stage.
>
> *Step 2*: They tell the target company of their intention to make an offer, usually with an indication of price.
>
> *Step 3*: Target accepts or rejects with reasons.
>
> *Step 4*: Negotiations over the price, Heads of Agreement agreed and eventually a final offer is made. The Board of the target will recommend acceptance or rejection.
>
> *Step 5*: Put to shareholders of target (this bit is always compulsory).
>
> *Step 6*: Regulatory authorities involved. In the UK the Office of Fair Trading may refer the deal to the Competition Commission. If the deal crosses into other EU countries the EU Merger Task Force may be involved. If a US company is involved the Securities and Exchange Commission may also need to give approval. In many industries there are also industry specific bodies, such as the Food and Drug Administration (FDA) in the USA for food or drug companies, or the various government watchdogs in the UK, for example, Oftel for the telecoms industry.
>
> *Step 7*: Completion.

There are two huge communication challenges connected with a contested or lengthy bidding process. The first is that it often takes months. Meanwhile business as usual must continue, and the communicator has the ongoing task of maintaining enthusiasm about current plans and projects – even though everyone knows that these might change if the deal goes ahead. Throughout this period there are extremely stringent confidentiality issues concerning the deal, which boil down to the fact that you can only tell employees what is already in the public domain – for example copies of letters to shareholders and defence documents on your website.

The second challenge is the long-lasting effect on credibility of an extended bidding process. Through the long period of defence the target will be trying to show the world that it can go ahead successfully independently. It may even be publishing derogatory comments about the bidder and its suitability as an owner of this sort of business. When, later and usually at a different price, the deal does go ahead there is a new message about how much better off the companies will be together. There is little you can do about this as an internal communicator. Your best plan is to keep to the relevant topics outside the deal, topics where you can build real credibility and to which employees' own work is devoted, for instance changes in the marketplace, new contracts and organisational successes at a local level.

Contingency Planning for Leaks

The Takeover Code is clear that negotiations and plans should be secret until the bidder is in a position to state its intention of making a bid. It is, however, realistic about the need to make an announcement should "rumour and speculation" be rife, particularly if it affects the share price. In practice this means that both parties need to be prepared for a leak and to have to go public at short notice.

This contingency planning will of course cover a range of audiences, especially the City and the financial press; you need to make sure that it covers employees in your organisation, too. In order to do this you need to be able to contact employees quickly in all locations, and you need to arrange for senior managers to be spoken to personally.

In accordance with Stock Exchange rules only a tiny number of insiders on each side will know of the potential deal. Senior managers who have given years of their lives to the organisation, and who identify with it closely, may well feel betrayed and undermined by hearing about an issue facing their organisation from the public media. Their colleagues inside the organisation and contacts outside it will expect them, as senior people, to know what is going on. It is essential that you reach such people as soon as possible, planning phone calls from the few insiders to the 20 or 30 people who will feel mortified if there is no conversation with them. You need to make sure that each of the insiders has his or her own list of who to call and what their mobile numbers are so that they can reach them quickly in the event of a leak. They need to have an agreed text about what to say, including the inability to say much for legal reasons and, if possible, some idea of the likely timetable or at least the next steps.

Of course, if you yourself know nothing of the offer until you see or hear it in the press, you cannot do much contingency planning. As mentioned in Stage One, you need to make sure at least that you have the contact details, typically the mobile phone numbers, of all your senior managers so that they can be reached wherever they are in the world. You may already have this as part of your generic disaster plan.

If the leak has come from the bidder's side at an early stage it is possible that no one in the target side knows of the potential offer before they see it in the public media. A generic disaster communication plan can prove its worth at such a time.

Communication During Negotiations

If the deal is contested there is likely to be much public speculation about the prospect and much written about the two organisations. Both sides will prepare documents about how they see the future of their company, with or without the deal. This stage is challenging for the internal communicator for three reasons. First, the critical power of the bidder may have galvanised the target into outlining future strategy more explicitly than formerly. The content of the defence document can include new information deeply interesting to employees, for example outlining implicitly or explicitly possible cost-savings to be made by cutting the number of employees. If there are plans for cost-cutting you need to make sure they are communicated in the usual way to employees, rather than letting them see comments or documents in the public domain and drawing their own conclusions.

Second, these documents are usually produced at great speed and intensity, giving you little time to plan or execute internal communication. Third, lawyers will be particularly keen that no new or different information is given to employees from that in the defence document, which will be written in a jargon impenetrable to all but a tiny proportion of employees.

 All you can do is make sure that you are at the drafting table and able to alert colleagues about internal implications of the document; make sure you have a good, quick means of communicating what comes out; and warn employees that regulatory limitations make it hard to use words other than those in the statements themselves. A further piece of advice from communicators who have been through this stage is to make sure that the most senior people in the organisation are willing to stand up to lawyers for obtaining quick clearance and intelligible announcements.

Good example of quick employee communication

The London Stock Exchange used "Skinkers" (a form of pop-up desk-top alert) to let employees know immediately when there was a development in the long-running takeover saga at the London Stock Exchange before its merger with Borsa Italiana in October 2007.

PREPARING FOR THE ANNOUNCEMENT

You face another set of challenges as you prepare for the initial announcement. First impressions are vital. You only get one chance at the announcement, and the emotive nature of any potential loss of identity to an organisation makes people sensitive to the slightest nuance or infelicity of tone. In addition, you are limited as to the content of your communication, not only from legal restraints but because many answers to even the most basic and obvious of questions are not yet known.

Agreeing the Statement between the Parties

It is hugely helpful if there is an agreed and common statement from both parties about the proposed deal. Obviously at this stage the respective communication teams will not yet have had a chance to plan extensively together, but thinking through the immediate announcement to the various audiences is essential. People will know former colleagues, suppliers or customers in the other organisation and will compare notes about the message. Consistency is therefore essential.

It can be particularly hard to get the tone right if there has been a long and quite public battle, especially if the target's argument has centred on the suitability of the fit or the quality or record of the bidder management. There may have been press releases by each side denigrating the other: the bidder claiming that the current management has not served shareholders well and has not maximised the assets of the organisation; and the target claiming that the bidder is undervaluing the company and even that they would be unsuitable owners. In a hostile or contested bid it is likely that the target will have communicated as actively as it can that it has a lively and uniquely successful plan for growth as an independent entity. The contradictions between these statements and the later recommendation to go ahead with the deal can be difficult to reconcile. Pride on the part of both parties may make this a hard statement to draft. It will also be written with external stakeholders in mind. Your job is to make sure that the internal audience for this statement is not forgotten.

Clarity of Objective and Future Measurement

We have already seen the need to be clear about the strategic objectives of any acquisition and the role of the internal communicator in helping the top team to share their aspirations. With an actual deal in sight more specific objectives for the deal can be set, and again it is the communicator's job to make sure that these objectives are more than an empty shell of words. It can be useful to think of the objectives from the point of view of various key stakeholders. For example, what might be the objectives for shareholders, for lenders, for customers and for employees. These should be in measurable terms. This obviously requires you to work closely with colleagues responsible for communication with these various groups.

The Various Audiences

One of the features of the press coverage that both parties to the deal need to consider is their response to the inevitable questions about potential job losses. This is an angle which the press will take, and your line should be agreed. In the absence of convincing data or reasons why nothing can yet be decided, there is every likelihood of journalists guessing about job losses. They are often interpreting statements in the full financial documents about potential savings. If your statements mention integration savings it is important to be as explicit as possible about how much, if any, of the saving is likely to be on people.

Among employees, the means and nuance of the message should be varied according to different segments of the audience. You will need to think about giving any employee who has contact with external stakeholders information, and even on occasions a text, for their conversations with stakeholders. Most obviously, this is the case for customer-facing staff. It can be as important to tell people what *not* to say as what to say. Where the announcement is likely to be big news, either nationally or locally, all employees will need guidance about what to say to family, friends and neighbours. When planning the communication to various stakeholders, you need to think about the alternative channels that are used as well as the principal ones.

In addition to the usual stakeholders of shareholders, customers, suppliers, joint-venture partners, local communities, NGOs and so on, an important audience for announcements which is often forgotten is alumni. Whether they are pensioners or people who have been with you before pursuing their careers elsewhere, they are likely to have views about the organisation and some are likely to be deemed authoritative by current colleagues, friends and family. What they think of the deal matters. They may well have ongoing social relations with current employees, and have an influence on their views. In many cases ongoing poison from alumni can sour relations in the new organisation. While messages of hope about the new organisation may elicit enthusiasm from current employees, former ones have no stake in the organisation's future.

The only stake ex-employees may have in the organisation is their pensions. They may have been worried about the former organisation going under and discontinuing the scheme, or they may be worried that a future employer is more likely to do so. Aside from pension considerations they may fear that the name with which they were associated might disappear and that the organisation where they continue perhaps to have some social contact might become unrecognisable. There is nothing but loss for them here. If you are able to communicate with them, perhaps through addresses via the pension fund, it is worth taking the trouble to do so.

Increasingly, organisations are starting to take their alumni seriously as an audience. Thomson Group, for example, has a section on its website for alumni, acknowledging their ongoing emotional engagement with the group and their power as potential ambassadors and informal recruiters. If you have reached this stage in the deal and you have no alumni network of any sort, you might be a little too busy on other things to set one up now, but it is worth doing in less frantic times.

Subcontractors, freelancers and temps working in the business can also be influential. They are sometimes more worldly-wise than other employees, having seen more places of work. It is worth minimising their cynicism and making sure that they are included in communication to all staff.

Communication Planning

The practical issue of planning will include thinking about channels, timing and segmenting the audience. It is worth detailing for each audience what they are likely to be receiving when. There is of course considerable overlap between audiences: for example many employees may be shareholders; shareholders will read the general press. It can be revealing to contrast the messages being given in the different media and think it through from the point of view of an individual stakeholder.

Explaining the Rationale for the Deal

The fundamental question which all the stakeholders want answered is: why will one organisation do better in any way than the previous separate ones? The answer may differ in detail and emphasis from audience to audience, but the fundamental message needs to be the same and needs to reflect a vision for the new organisation. One of the communication challenges at this period is likely to be the lawyers' fears of breaching Stock Exchange regulations by giving one party more information about the possible deal than another. By planning communication to the various audiences together, this problem can be overcome.

One of the challenges about communicating the rationale for the deal is that mergers and acquisitions often happen when a particular market is in turmoil, either because of technological or regulatory change, or because there is overcapacity in the market. It can therefore be difficult for leaders to paint a realistic picture of the new organisation and its place in the market.

Consider the holiday and tours industry in 2007. In an ex growth market several companies decided to merge in order to benefit from the cost savings which shunting two businesses together can generate. Little thought may have been given to what will actually reactivate a mature market. The pressure not to be left out was paramount. After completion employees naturally wanted to know that there was more to the merger than just "consolidation". That's fine as a table stake but consolidation to do what? Where are the "sunlit uplands", Where is the business going? Just consolidating does not mean that a mature market can be reinvigorated.

One of the key messages you need to convey in the announcement is the competence of the new organisation. As we have seen trust is built from perceptions of competence and integrity. Employee views on the competence of the new top team are built from the first announcement. Having muddled logic or incorrect facts will deal a blow to trust which will last a long time.

The risk of perceived incompetence

People in Business was called into one organisation some 18 months after an internal merger. A common gripe among the intelligent and professional workforce was that they still could not see the reason for the merger, and that the announcement had never really explained why the parent company was merging these subsidiaries. Not only did this mean they had little tolerance for any inconveniences caused by the merger, but they had no trust in the top management, whom they perceived as incompetent, largely because they had not succeeded in communicating a rationale for the merger.

Getting the language right

All words are shot through with intentions and accents ... Each word tastes of the contexts in which it has lived its socially charged life.

Bakhtin

As far as internal audiences are concerned, it is important to remember that not all employees understand management jargon. While it is acceptable to use similar language when speaking to financial audiences and senior management, as soon as you are talking to a wider range of employees you need to be aware that they may not necessarily understand financial terms.

Inappropriate financial jargon

In one organisation employing research scientists, most of whom had PhDs, the company sent the same communication to its internal audience as to the financial stakeholders, on the grounds that its employees were intelligent people. The scientists, however, had little knowledge of or interest in financial and City terminology. They soon stopped reading the announcements on the grounds that they did not understand them, and waited for the grapevine to give them the low-down on what was really happening.

It is worth checking out draft statements with non-managers if possible before the announcement, as you may well find you are insensitive to words which are in everyday use in senior management circles but have a quite different meaning, or none at all, to other readers.

> ### The dangers of management jargon
>
> One organisation wanted to stress the fact that the future organisation would
> not have internal boundaries and referred to "silos". Feedback afterwards from IT
> professionals who were the audience was that they were not farmers and had no
> idea what the Chief Executive was talking about!

It is worth remembering what different resonance words have for different
individuals and different sectors of your audience. Think about the
vocabulary used in previous announcements and change programmes; be
aware that the words will carry meaning forward, for better or worse. In one
organisation, for example, the word "change" itself had come to mean "job
losses", and communication had to be drafted avoiding the loaded word.

When people are upset or shocked, their ability to process information is
diminished. This not only means that information needs to be available for
people to read at their leisure, when they are ready to take it in, but it also
influences how the message is conveyed in the first place. There needs to be
some repetition of the main points. Covello et al. (2001) also suggest that
people who are upset are likely to think negatively, so it is important to avoid
words like "not" or "never".

Table 3.1   Dos and don'ts of language

Do	Don't
Use consistent language across the audiences for the main concepts, for example, is it a merger or an acquisition? The same phrase about the main purpose needs to be repeated constantly.	Use the word merger if it is really an acquisition. If you do it is likely to cause cynicism later when the real nature of the deal becomes clear.
Use positive language about the potential for the new organisation.	Use negative words such as "not", "never", and so on.
Use positive but realistic language, for example, "we are going to become part of …".	Use negative language, for example, "we are being taken over by …".
Keep talking about the external challenges the new organisation faces and why the new organisation is better placed than its predecessors to meet them.	Denigrate either of the old organisations or their previous management teams. The more the need for change can be presented as the response to changing circumstances or a way of seizing opportunities the better.

Merger or acquisition?

One of the aspects of the announcement message which must be absolutely clear is the nature of the deal. Is it a merger or an acquisition? Genuine mergers are extremely rare; more often than not there is an obvious and real leading partner, even if the financial deal is not simply an acquisition. It is important not to be misleading about this. In some cases long-term cynicism about subsequent company announcements can be traced back to talk of a "merger of equals" at the announcement stage, which was followed by a series of other announcements and actions which made it clear that one party was dominant. Inevitably people will be scrutinising every decision and action to try to interpret which party is dominant. This is particularly clear once decisions begin to be made about which of the former company's processes or customs to follow.

LOGISTICS OF THE INITIAL ANNOUNCEMENT

Whatever the particular channels and angles your communication plan suggests, one key plank is likely to be the announcement, made as quickly as possible in each of your locations.

In order to reach office-based people as soon as possible, it is usual to email *everyone* – preferably with a link from the homepage of the intranet – with a short announcement and an invitation to attend meetings within the next few hours where they will have the opportunity of hearing more about the deal and have a chance to ask questions.

Getting the length of the email right is a balancing act between putting in enough information to quell the grapevine but having a short enough announcement that people are likely to read it and not rely on colleagues to read it and tell them what it says. Our advice is to have the top line facts and dates, along with a couple of sentences on the rationale, and encourage people to come to the meetings (or receive the satellite broadcasts) to hear more. Too much detail at this stage will detract from the message. People should, however, be able to access press releases and announcements to shareholders on the intranet.

At this stage there will have to be two internal communication plans: one for each of the former companies. Both have in common the need to communicate fast. Normally announcements of intent are made to the Stock Exchange at 07.30 in the morning. This can pose challenges for your internal communication if the deal is sufficiently big to make the national or local news; there is a danger that employees will hear about the intent on the television while they are getting up or on the radio as they drive to work.

The Importance of Timing

> When Aviva was formed from the previous Norwich Union and CGU in February 2000 the announcement to the Stock Exchange was delayed until 09.30 in order to allow employees to be told at the same time.

Because of time differences around the world it may not be possible, even with every effort, to beat the public media to the announcement. This is one reason why it is so important in the run-up to the deal to explain to people what the process of acquisition is and why there will be silence followed by a sudden announcement. It can make people feel unvalued by their employer to hear of a major corporate development through the public media – or, worse still, through friends or family alerting them to the public media – but it helps if they knew it might happen.

Some organisations attempt to have the statement coincide with the announcement of regular results. This is hugely helpful as it means that all the logistics of arrangements can run as usual. It also means that there is a public reason for asking people to be prepared for a message or meeting, without alerting suspicion and setting the grapevine speculating.

> **The value of contingency planning**
>
> In one financial services deal, the acquisition was timed for the same moment as the announcement of the annual results. If the deal had been delayed there would have been no embarrassment of having to cancel venues for management meetings, and so on, since they would anyway have had the results to talk about.

Communicating the Announcement to your People

Within your own organisation you have readily available your own usual channels for communicating major pieces of corporate news. As far as possible people should be told quickly and face to face. It is a challenging logistical exercise to make sure that there are suitable arrangements at every site. What is more it is a difficult balancing act deciding how much freedom to give local managers in the communication. On the one hand, giving them too much freedom may lead to some deciding not to communicate at all or to give their own individualistic version (a prospect your lawyers will hate). On the other, having too rigid a process and message can prevent local managers dealing with issues which they know will be important to people and using channels they know will work for them.

The extent to which detailed communication plans need to be made is obviously affected by the likely impact of the deal on people, or their likely perceptions of the deal on them. However, our experience is that it is better to err on the side of over-communicating than under-communicating. Once the initial message has been received, by channels you have initiated or through public media or the grapevine, the tone is set for future announcements. If you have failed to seize the initiative at the announcement stage, you may find yourself playing catch-up later. The worst that can happen if you make a real effort to communicate a deal which people think has only marginal interest to them is that they will think you have wasted some time and money. The worst that can happen if you fail to make the effort to communicate actively with everyone is that they can feel resentful and suspicious from the start.

On the other hand, you need to keep the communication in perspective for the particular audiences site-by-site. The chances are that there are many other messages of more immediate impact on employees' productivity or effectiveness. At least one version of the script or presentation for managers may need to be very short if the audience is unlikely to be impacted much and/or to have little interest in the announcement.

The practicalities of the announcement are, of course, much easier if people are employed at a few large sites with communication professionals present and with good communication infrastructure such as the ability to web-cast, theatres where people can hear satellite announcements, and so on. In many cases, however, you also need to consider smaller sites where the local management will have no professional support on-hand and maybe few technological tools.

Preparing smaller sites for the announcement may involve:

- Alerting the local management to the fact that some urgent communication may come in the next few days.

- Making sure they have adequate plans for receiving the information confidentially. For example, do they personally receive email or do their emails go to a secretary in a general office; are they equipped to receive password-protected emails and if so, what is the password to be? If there is no email access to some sites, it may be necessary to prepare managers to wait by fax machines at a certain time.

- Making sure that the senior person is actually going to be on-site at the relevant time, or, if not, that there is a nominated deputy who knows what to do. It can be a disaster if you email the depot or branch manager but it turns out he or she is on holiday and no one else has access to their email.

- Making sure they are ready to run face-to-face sessions where possible, but, if not, distributing through noticeboards or email.

- Making sure that they have ways of reaching all employees based at their site, whether or not they work there every day. Sales people who work from home, drivers and repair engineers are among the groups of people who may have a nominal local office or depot but in practice start and finish each working day at home. A manager has the responsibility of making sure each of these people has been told and has access to all the available information.

- Making sure shift-workers and part-timers, who may not be due at the site for a number of days, can be told by telephone or as soon as they come in for work.

- Finding out what facilities the site has for communication. For example do they have the ability to project using a PowerPoint presentation, or should you provide overhead transparencies or even flipchart pages?

At larger sites it may involve:

- Having the senior people as insiders (this is typically only the case where it has been necessary for the preliminary due diligence).

- Booking meeting rooms.

- Alerting people to come to meetings on the relevant days, even though you cannot tell them what the announcement is about.

- Arranging satellite links with simultaneous broadcasts in different sites, possibly across different continents, if this is the way you usually communicate.

- Of course it is hard to do any of this if you have almost no notice of the announcement yourself. What you can do, however, is to have generic crisis or urgent communication plans in place into which this announcement can fall.

Depending on the nature and size of the acquisition, bidder employees may or may not themselves feel threatened by the proposed deal. Experience suggests that acquiring employees often feel less threatened than they should. People sometimes prefer not to think that they might be negatively impacted. We quite often find that when acquirer employees lose out in the integration projects (for instance if work is moved to a former target's site), they are shocked and feel betrayed.

Communicating the Announcement to the Other Party's People

Within the other organisation you do not have any control over the means of communication, since often you will only have met your opposite number a matter of days, or at the most two or three weeks, before the announcement. You may not even have met them at all if the communication follows a leak or if you have not been an insider.

They will have their own tried-and-tested means of communicating to staff and now is not the moment to start experimenting with new ways. You can of course tell the other side about your own plans and they may well want to use some of the same logistical framework.

The value of collaboration in communications

One software company has a well-established process for managing acquisitions. It has a public strategy that it will expand, partly by acquisition. It is often quicker for the company to bring new products to market by buying the companies that develop them than to develop them from scratch themselves.

Most of the organisations they buy are very small, with between five and fifty employees. The process in these cases is that the people in financial, public relations and internal communications work closely together on the initial announcements to make sure that the rationale is clear and consistent between the audiences. The message to the new staff has the same rationale but may have additional topics of interest to an internal audience, such as benefits and organisational information.

On the day of the announcement the main communication is about the rationale for the purchase. A business review is also always announced together with its timetable, which is 30 or 60 days, depending on the size of the business. The business review is carried out by the buyer in partnership with the new business's management team. It is a rigorous review of the whole organisation, at the end of which changes are announced.

Table 3.2   Pros and cons of having bidder's senior people at large target sites

Pros	Cons
Shows commitment to the new organisation.	Can seem to disempower the local management; people may infer that they could not be trusted to put across the message without Big Brother looking over their shoulder.
Can answer questions.	Unlikely to know the local situation or audience well enough to strike the right note.
Shows a human face, preventing some of the demonisation of the acquiring organisation which can otherwise happen.	Logistically difficult, since the same people may be needed at the bidder's own sites if the deal is a big one for the bidder.
Can be most useful when the old entity is likely to be subsumed completely into the new one, for example, when the acquirer is much bigger and frequently makes this sort of acquisition.	Can be least useful when none of the answers about the future are yet known, and where it is possible that not much will change on the site.

As we have seen, the one element which must be coordinated is the message, which needs to be substantially the same, though obviously targeted for the different audiences. There will be informal contacts across the two organisations at all levels, even at this stage, with people knowing each other through previous employment, training or social contact. People *will* compare notes.

It is sometimes helpful if, even at this stage, there are some senior people from the bidder at the announcements on large target sites.

It is important, anyway, that the meeting is led by people's own senior managers, who are seen to be giving the message. This will add credibility and impart a sense of continuity and show that the employees have not just been abandoned by their previous management. Even if the target's management team have already made the decision to leave the new company (or they have been told they will not be required), they should at least introduce the acquirer's management team and endorse the deal.

There is a related issue for the announcement, which is about preserving the self-esteem of the target's employees. In some cases there is a real failure of the target that lies behind the acquisition. The target organisation may:

- have over-extended;
- be unable to grow without expertise or other resources from a parent;
- have failed to capitalise on a tangible or intangible asset;
- be unable to offer the sort of career structure necessary to keep the people it needs;
- be unable to grasp opportunities because of a lack of specific competence or skill;
- be creaking administratively and starting to let down customers or be blacklisted by suppliers;
- have run out of energy and creativity and be coasting along on old products or services.

In any of these cases there may be a genuine view that the previous management has failed the organisation, and some of the more junior managers or front-line staff may also be implicated. There may be some justification, in other words, for their current sense of inferiority. While it is important to be honest about the reasons for the deal, it is equally important to help people preserve their pride. If employees feel that their noses are being rubbed in their failures they tend to become resentful and unwilling to cooperate.

The target management is likely to be in an awkward position when leading these meetings. They may have in their mind one of the following thoughts about their own futures:

- I am definitely leaving this organisation, by my decision or theirs. I do not have a future here and my successful days here are over.

- I do not know what my future holds and I am worried about it.

- This is a great move forward for me personally. I can have a more exciting and more lucrative future with this new organisation than the old one.

And one or more of the following is likely to be in their minds about the reception they expect from their employees:

- I feel I have failed these people and if I had been cleverer at my job we might not have come to this, and we might even be buying someone else now.

- The employees will wrongly think I have failed them, but actually this is the best thing for them as the new organisation has *[whatever resources or skills]* that we didn't have.

- Employees probably are thinking that this is the beginning of the end for this site, and they are probably right.

- Employees probably are thinking that this is the beginning of the end for this site, but they are probably wrong.

- Employees will be delighted because this is not the closure that the grapevine has been predicting for this site (or at least not yet).

- Employees will be comparing this announcement to the previous time we were bought, when the acquirer promised investment and development which we never received. They won't believe a word of this.

The bidder of course is unlikely to know which of these fears are playing in people's heads. It is therefore important to help the target's managers decide exactly how these meetings should be held in the target organisation.

In a merger or acquisition of similar size organisations, the same fears may be playing in the heads of buyer employees, and again local management should be involved in deciding the method and detail of the message.

Which Media to Use for the Announcement

It is useful to segment the audience by the degree to which they are likely to be affected and whether or not the deal is likely to be publicly communicated. Different segments have different needs (see Table 3.3).

Table 3.3   Which media to use for which audience

Audience characteristic	Channel to use
Unlikely to hear from public media and unlikely to be affected directly.	Pull channels, for example, intranet site and in-house magazine.
Unlikely to be affected directly but will hear company's name on public media.	Can still use relatively "lean" channels, that is, little need for feedback, but need to make sure that everyone is the recipient of active communication, for example, email to all staff, notice on boards, front page of intranet.
May be affected or think themselves affected.	Active face-to-face channels needed. People need to hear about the deal with as much detail as possible, have the chance to air their concerns and ask questions, even if you have few answers at this stage. You may need to balance the level from which people need to hear with the desire for face-to-face communication.

CONTENT OF THE ANNOUNCEMENT PACK

The packs for 'A' day included feedback requests and asked people what they were concerned about and what they wanted to know more about. This was useful data in the subsequent communication.

Aviva

Managers making the announcement, in whichever company, will need an announcement pack. The amount of detail in the pack will vary according to how much work has been done before this first announcement, and how much notice you have to prepare it. It may be that it can only say that the parties have agreed to investigate the case and hope to make a deal; it may be that some of the major decisions about the new organisation have already been made and are merely subject to shareholder and/or regulatory approval. In this case it may be possible to announce the top team of the new organisation, and even something of its structure below that. In some cases it may be possible to make announcements about the future of sites.

One of the principles underlying your decisions about the pack is that it should make communication as easy as possible for the many busy managers who will have to do the communicating. They have their own day-to-day concerns as well as the corporate communication job you are asking of them. The easier you make the pack to use, the more likely local managers are to use it and to do the job well.

It is therefore important that the manager's pack is well indexed and that materials are produced in whatever form is most helpful to them, whether this be PowerPoint, overhead transparencies or flipchart posters. It is helpful to provide scripts rather than just notes. If managers choose to elaborate or use their own words they will, but if there is a script you can be sure that the least confident or energetic manager will at least have the means to run a successful communication session.

The dangers of early announcements about senior people

In one acquisition in the retail industry two directors of the target were initially named as joining the bidder's board; later this decision was reversed as they were let go quite quickly after the new board was formed. When the reverse was announced it initially had a demotivating impact on other senior people in the target, who interpreted the departures as evidence that people from the target would not be valued in the new company.

Checklist: Content of the Manager's Pack

Depending on the degree of detail available, the manager's pack should ideally include the following:

- Personal note from the leader of the new organisation (if known) or if not from the two leaders of the former organisations which sets out the rationale for the deal.

- Brief histories and descriptions of the two organisations and why they will make good partners.

- Any decisions already made about the future shape or management of the new organisation.

- The structure and management of the project of merging or integrating the acquisition if you have got that far. If possible name the leaders of workstreams, but, if not, at least list workstreams if they have been agreed; or if you are not yet even at that stage then list the senior executives who will be making the decisions about how to manage the merger.

- Any promises or guarantees to employees that you wish to make. Be wary of making any promises – it may well be, once the full due diligence is done and possibly as late as halfway through the integration projects, that you need to change your mind. Assurances that all sites will be kept open or that there will be no compulsory redundancies may prove to be hostages to fortune. There are often conflicting pressures on the communicator at this stage. On the one hand, you do not want to make promises you later have to break; on the other, you are aware that your competitors and their headhunters will be on the look-out for some of your best professional and managerial talent, and that some of these people may start brushing up their CVs if the outlook does not look rosy in the new entity. There is also the natural human desire to please, and therefore to tell people what they want to hear.

• Any other substantive decisions which have already been taken in the early negotiations, such as the name of the new organisation and where the Head Office will be situated, which is often an emotive issue.

• Copies of communication to other key audiences, for example press releases, note to shareholders.

• Q&As to address the most likely questions. You need to give managers the assurance that you have thought of these questions, even if the answer to most of the questions is that it is too early to say.

• The subsequent process and timetable so far as possible. In most cases there is a need for regulatory approval, and that can take longer than anticipated. At this stage you are therefore unlikely to be able to offer a definite timetable. If you are not anticipating delays from the regulatory authorities it may be possible to give a tentative one. In any case it is essential to spell out what the regulatory process is, as well as future stages of due diligence that will dictate whether or not the deal actually goes through, if that is relevant.

• If you know it already, it is helpful to tell people about the process by which the top jobs in the new company will be filled and, if possible, how subsequent levels of management will be decided.

• Where to go for further information, while making it clear that there is not much detail available at this stage. If possible there should be an email helpline or staffed telephone line, open at least for the first few days.

• Information about what to say externally and what not to say. Who enquiries should be addressed to (typically the Press Office).

• It is useful to make it clear right from the outset whether acquiring company people can all expect automatically to keep their jobs, or whether they will have to compete with the target people where there are duplications. It is also helpful if you can give some idea of which sites are likely to remain open, or at least what the decision-making process is likely to be.

• If TUPE regulations apply, it is worth outlining the implications. If they do not, it is worth saying why not, as otherwise people may assume they do.

• Information about future communication: how and when employees will be informed of decisions as they emerge and how they can pose questions or express opinions.

- Guidelines for managers on how to run break-out sessions. The purpose of the break-out sessions is for people to start to think through the implications. In some cases these sessions can be run by managers within their departments; in others more senior people can run them with mixed groups of people. One of the useful questions to ask people in these sessions is what they already know or have heard about the other party to the deal. It is important to collect this information so that your subsequent communication is appropriate. It can also be a useful source of information as an informal part of due diligence.

If possible it is worth exchanging drafts of all this material with the other party to the deal to check that there are no inconsistencies.

**How one financial services company handled
an acquisition of a competitor**

The announcement in the bidder organisation

The very first communication was a holding email first thing in the morning, acknowledging that people would have heard the announcement on the breakfast news and telling them that there would be briefings for the rest of the day. It told them what they should say to customers and where they should direct press enquiries.

It was arranged that one of the very senior managers would be at each site to brief managers. There were full packs for the briefers, including Q&As, among them an explanation for why people could not have been told earlier. The briefing packs also gave the reasons for the acquisition, background on the two companies, an explanation of what would happen next, why it would go so quiet and some headlines anticipating which parts of the business it would affect the most (for example, back office functions). Middle managers were later given the same briefing packs to brief their own teams.

The logistics of getting people taken off the phones were challenging, as many were in call centres. The Internal Communication Manager was able to engage the help of Resource Planning, but it was hard to do so given that she could not tell them why they needed to plan the briefings. She had to say things to them like "You need to think about what you would do if we had to..."

The announcement the same day in the target

There was a fuller written brief emailed to everyone.

The group CEO of the bidder conducted a presentation and Q&A session at the target's main site. This session was videoed and the videos sent round the various locations.
Meanwhile in the target organisation communication followed their regular pattern for major announcements, that is, a personal email from the target's CEO (and founder).

> **How Pfizer successfully communicated the acquisition of Pharmacia**
>
> The announcement was made internally by video satellite to all locations, with the CEOs of both organisations on the platform. The central communication team in New York had worked all weekend so that when the UK Research Internal Communication Manager arrived at work on the Monday morning there was a message asking him to set up the video conference and a package of material for him to use. The announcement had been leaked the night before.
> About 200 people of the 2,500 on site turned up to the broadcast. Other communication included:
>
> - an email direct from CEO to all 80,000 email boxes in the company;
>
> - a special edition of the global web-based newsletter (normally fortnightly), including messages to investors and a summary of the intent announcement speeches, mainly about the rationale for the acquisition.

What the Recipients of the Message Hear

Different internal audiences will have different frames of reference into which they receive communication. The tone and vocabulary used in the initial announcement is also immensely important influencing in the way all subsequent messages will be heard. As we have seen, the message will be heard differently by different people, depending on their previous associations with the words and concepts the announcement evokes. For everyone, though, there are two considerations which will dominate their thinking, and which should therefore influence the announcement's content and tone.

1. What's this going to mean for me personally?

2. How does this compare with the last time something similar happened?

Let's look more closely at each of these in turn.

What's in it for me personally?

Every recipient, from the most senior to the most junior, will have two records playing in their head as they listen to the announcement: what difference will this make to the organisation and its customers, and what difference will this make to me? The personal questions playing in people's heads are likely to be:

- Will I keep my job?

- If so will my job change a lot?

- Will I be able to cope with the changes in my job?

- Will I keep my work companions and colleagues?

- Will I keep my boss?

- Will I have to move location?

- What does this mean for my prospects of promotion?

- Will my pay and/or the basis for my pay and pay increases change?

- What affect will this have on my pension? (This is a really important one for certain audiences, and you should have as much information as possible about pensions or the process by which the pension decisions will be taken.)

- Will I be able to keep any particular personal advantages I have managed to negotiate with my boss, the organisation or colleagues informally?

Of course you are unlikely to be able to answer any of these questions at this stage. It is worth telling people that you know these thoughts are in their minds, though. These are the parts of the announcement to which people will listen, and having earned their attention by covering the areas they are interested in, you are more likely to get them to hear the rest of the presentation. The more you can tell people the better, even if it is only about the process by which such things will be decided and the likely outline timetable.

On the other hand, it is important that the business rationale of the deal is explained and is available for people to come back to. An adult-to-adult tone in communication demands that the hard business realities are faced; in the long run it does no one any favours to treat employees as children who need to be protected from harsh truths and told only about the matters that concern them.

As well as the personal questions people will be asking themselves, there will also be specific business questions, such as:

- Does this mean the planned investment in *[whatever]* will happen? (This may be particularly important to managers and professionals who are deeply immersed in a project.)

- Will this affect the changes in organisation that we have been talking about?

- Will this affect relationships with suppliers or customers with whom I deal all the time and whose relationship is important to me?

- Will it change how work is organised or allocated?

Again, you are most unlikely to be able to answer most of these questions at this stage, but it is worth considering what the questions are likely to be for different audiences. If there are major changes affecting a number of people, for example, a new IT system in the offing, it is worth thinking carefully about what you can say about it. Again, just acknowledging that you know and care what people are concerned about is in itself an important message.

How does this compare with the last time something similar happened?

This is slightly more complicated, as there is more variation. Memories of past mergers and acquisitions live long. In one case we were involved in there were ongoing grievances and disputes, both formal and informal, from an acquisition seven years earlier. Everything that people in that organisation heard about the new merger went through a filter of their memories of the badly handled one seven years earlier. Even new people were aware of it, partly because the company used rosters of staff which referred to people by their staff numbers as well as their names and they had kept distinct staff numbers for employees of the acquired company, so people were reminded of their legacy organisation. You must refer to previous mergers or acquisitions explicitly and make such distinctions or comparisons as are necessary. If you do not, people will assume, for better or worse, that this one will be similar, and all the emotions and resentments caused by that deal will be transferred wholesale to this one.

Even if there is no history of corporate change in either organisation, there is almost certain to be a memory of some major announcement from their current employer. It may be of a site closure or major restructuring or even good news relating to a major investment decision. One reason why it is worth leaving some of the detail of how to communicate up to local managers is that they are likely to know what sort of things most of their audience will be remembering, and be able to make the necessary connections or distinctions.

COMMUNICATING WITH UNIONS

It is important to inform the unions in advance of the announcement. Organisations are often nervous about doing this, for fear of leaks. In our research we have often come across leaks, but never have they been blamed on the unions. Under the Stock Exchange regulations it is permissible to inform Officials of Unions in confidence about prospective changes. The usual practice is to tell the general secretaries or other very senior union people on the eve of the announcement, but a number of interviewees said in retrospect that they wished they had informed them earlier.

KEY PLAYERS

At this stage there will be considerable contact with your most senior management who will be involved in the announcements; there may be some contact with senior managers from the other party.

Key contacts for you at this stage will be other communicators working with external audiences such as investor relations and public relations. You may also be working with colleagues in IT over practical arrangements like satellite links and podcasts.

WHAT SORT OF LISTENING TO DO AT THIS STAGE

At this stage you can only do fairly passive listening, as there will still be mainly questions without answers. There are two main topics for listening:

- Asking employees about their previous experiences with or opinions about the new partner. This is helpful as it may give you information to feed into due diligence about which you may have been ignorant. It also gives you an insight into employees' current levels of knowledge and how positive they are about the partner, which will help you have the right tone and content in your further communication about them.

- Particular concerns of employees, not just about their individual circumstances, in particular pensions and career possibilities, but also more short-term business concerns which may get forgotten as so much management effort is diverted into the deal and into planning for Day One.

WHAT EMPLOYEES ARE THINKING AND SAYING

What You Want Them to be Thinking and Saying

Let's wait and hear what impact this will have. Let's get on with business as usual in the meantime.

Whether or not it will be good for me, I can see that it's the right thing for the company.

What You Don't Want Them to be Thinking and Saying

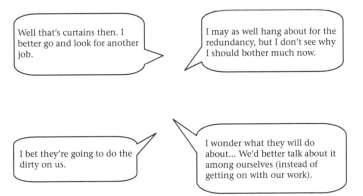

> Well that's curtains then. I better go and look for another job.

> I may as well hang about for the redundancy, but I don't see why I should bother much now.

> I bet they're going to do the dirty on us.

> I wonder what they will do about... We'd better talk about it among ourselves (instead of getting on with our work).

THE COST OF GETTING IT WRONG

- The main cost of getting it wrong is having the wrong sort of listening established from then on among employees. If the tone or message strikes the wrong note then all subsequent communication will be pushing against some misconceptions which may prove hard to shift.

- If you fail to inform the unions of the proposed deal you risk earning their enmity to the deal and ongoing difficulties in relationships may ensue.

- On the other hand, if you make too much of a meal of communicating the announcement when there is little to say and most of your employees are unlikely to be affected, line managers or communicators around the business will develop the habit of ignoring material you send them.

SUMMARY FOR INTERNAL COMMUNICATORS

1. Remember that you never get a second chance at a first impression. The initial announcement is extremely important.

2. However, there is also a very difficult balancing act to be done between giving people as much information as you can, as they will be thirsty for it, and not creating hostages to fortune by giving information prematurely which later turns out to be wrong.

3. It is important to liaise as far as possible with your opposite number in the other organisation so that people comparing notes across the companies report having heard the same story.

4. Since this is a time when there is likely to be external publicity, it is particularly important to be working with your colleagues communicating externally at this stage.

4 Stage Four: From the Announcement to Day One

This is the stage when the deal is public but before the actual merger takes place. Usually there are three activities that take place simultaneously:

- Regulatory approval is sought. In the UK there is a gap of at least six weeks between announcement and merger. Sometimes it can be much longer, especially if US or EU authorities are involved as well.

- Further due diligence and negotiation is sometimes done, fixing the final terms of the deal. Sometimes this will have been done prior to the announcement.

- Preparation for the joining of the two organisations is started.

It is still possible, throughout this period, that the deal might not come to fruition. Regulatory approval may not be forthcoming or negotiations may break down. In this case, of course, all the work done in preparation will be wasted.

In many ways this is the hardest time for communicators. There is often very little to say. Lawyers will be anxious about saying anything that is not verifiable, and many decisions will be awaiting final approval anyway. Since you may not be able to confer with your opposite numbers it may be difficult to ensure consistency between your organisation and your partner's, and the decisions which people most want to hear about – those concerning themselves and their immediate colleagues – will almost certainly not yet have been taken. There will therefore be a thirst for communication which you will not be able to quench.

The internal communicator's priorities in this time are:

- maintaining morale and motivation during the period between the announcement and Day One, when there are bound to be more questions about the future than there are answers;

- developing communication skills for integration;

- planning the communication infrastructure for the new organisation (if possible);

- communicating about the other organisation;

- specific preparation for Day One;

- listening and consultation.

Although this can seem a frustrating time, with no action and few decisions, it is also a busy time for the communicator if you are using it fully for the priorities set out in this chapter.

MAINTAINING MORALE AND MOTIVATION

This is often particularly hard to do in the target organisation, where people fear that they will be the poor relations in the organisation and that their jobs may be at risk. Even if they keep their jobs they may be nervous that they will lose status or their confidence in carrying out their jobs. Many of the best people might start brushing up their CVs and headhunters will be circling. The danger is that people stop taking care of their day-to-day jobs and become diverted into exchanging rumours and speculation.

Your challenge is to counter this effect while having little weaponry in the shape of hard information or answers to individuals' concerns. The communication armoury you need at this time includes:

- Having channels through which you can communicate *quickly*, so that any news that does come out can be disseminated rapidly. This might include, for example, announcements from the regulators, appointments for the new organisation or decisions about the integration process. If people recognise that trustworthy information will always be with them soon, the rumours (though inevitable) will have less power to terrify or demotivate.

- Have channels that can *listen individually* to people's concerns. Many of these are likely to be about pensions, but are likely also to cover other personal issues, including career, stock options and other individual concerns. Even if there is no news it is helpful if people can have someone to talk to who has time to listen and tell them what little there is to know. The important thing is that an individual feels that someone cares.

- Have messages that include *processes* as soon as they are known. People will be thirsty for information about the extent of integration planned, news of the new organisation structure and how it will work, information about workstreams, how they are to work and who is to head them and, more than anything, about appointments and the process for making appointments. The transparency and apparent fairness of the appointments process will be watched carefully by employees, who will scrutinise announcements, looking for evidence of who is winning and who is losing and what the culture of the new organisation will be like. People will also be keen to see what sort of representation their organisation is getting on workstreams, and what the terms of reference of workstreams are.

- Give people information about how to continue their own *personal and professional development*. Whatever their future, inside the new organisation or not, it is in people's interests to make sure they have full and up-to-date knowledge and skills to equip them for a future career. If workloads in the organisation decrease during the period of waiting and uncertainty between the announcement and decisions being taken, this can be a good time to offer training and to demonstrate care for people.

- Give people information about the *partner organisation*. Rumours will abound about the new organisation if they have to fill an information vacuum; people will be desperate to know all about it. In particular they will want to know about:

  — its products, markets, suppliers and customers in order to make educated guesses about how the merger or acquisition will impact on them;

  — its locations and what work is done in them – again so that they can guess at the impact on them;

  — the culture and practices in the partner organisation. If they are similar to those in the old organisation then it is less likely that they will change in the new one;

  — the key personalities and their preferences, style and vision.

- People will be *googling* to search for information on the new partner. Your employees are bound to find any blogs from discontented employees or chat rooms for aggrieved customers, so it is important that you give them a fuller picture than they may otherwise obtain.

- Give people the best idea you have of the likely *regulatory process*. Since it is often hard to predict how long the regulatory process will take, it helps simply to inform people about the sort of decisions the regulator will be taking and what principles he will be using.

- As far as possible give people a *timetable* of the merger process up to and after Day One. If dates are impossible because of uncertainties over how the regulatory process will take, it may be possible to give an idea of Day One + by month or quarter.

Maintaining morale between the announcement and Day One

At Safeway, labour turnover actually fell in the stores following the announcement of the purchase by Morrisons. How did they achieve this?

First, Safeway recognised that, faced with prolonged uncertainty, people want as much information as you can give them about what happens next and how they personally will be affected. They want the opportunity to raise their own issues with someone who can give them answers. And, above all, they want reassurance that someone "up there" is going to look after their interests.

How did they put this into practice? These are just a few examples:

- They set up a help desk manned by a trained team of customer-service people. Originally they put in a voicemail and email system for questions but they took out the voicemail when staff told them they wanted someone to talk to. Most of the issues raised were personal.

- They set up a structure of Colleague Councils across the business, which enabled them to capture a lot of the concerns at both store and Head Office level and feed them through to the board. But they were action bodies as well and sorted out quite a lot of issues at site level.

- Members of these councils monitored morale every four weeks by using a common, short questionnaire. This enabled them to quickly pick up any dips in morale and react. For example, everyone knew that the Competition Commission was due to deliver its report on 12 August but a lot of people had assumed that they would immediately know the result and that would trigger action. In reality, the report had to go to the DTI, where it sat for six weeks until Trade and Industry Secretary Patricia Hewitt was ready to pronounce. Consequently when nothing appeared on 12 August, the morale monitor told them that morale generally was down. So they re-doubled their efforts to explain the process and reassure everyone that there was nothing untoward about this.

- Safeway already had a well-established practice of monthly open meetings for everyone on the Hayes Head Office site, at which they discussed the sales performance, celebrated successes by individuals, talked about new product launches and so on. These meetings were video-linked to all their major distribution depots and telephone linked to store managers. The chairman, the CEO and all board members attended.

- And, no less important, they ensured that all directors were visible – both in Hayes and around the stores.

Second, and perhaps paradoxically, they put a lot more effort into training and development. The problem with trying to maintain business as usual in conditions of extreme uncertainty is that everyone knows that the business is really quite different from what it was before. It was very clear from the outset that some activities in major functional divisions were going to fall away, particularly in Marketing, Store Format Development and Property. Long-term projects were abandoned and, as a result, some people quickly realised they were going to be under-employed. So the company offered them redundancy on favourable terms and around 100 people went – out of a total headcount on the Hayes site of around 1,800.

For the great majority who remained, training and development became a high priority and for very obvious reasons.

- Safeway introduced a programme called "Looking to the Future" to enable people to gain new skills.

- They also provided a personal assistance programme, run by an external agency, including independent financial advice both for those who wanted outplacement and for those who wanted to stay.

- Some individuals benefited from enlarging their roles as others left, which obviously gave them additional motivation and experience.

- And the company topped all this off with a new, short course in leadership skills for senior managers. The uncertainty surrounding the business meant that they had to redefine established criteria for effective leadership. These were then built into the reward system and managers were given bonuses according to how effectively they demonstrated these criteria.

Third, at a very early stage in the process Safeway identified around 300 key individuals in Head Office, plus a few out in the field, whose roles and personal skills made it absolutely necessary for them to be retained. So they increased their redundancy terms and paid them special retention bonuses. But these bonuses weren't just given away. They were linked to achieving individual performance targets.

Finally, the company kept up its external profile so that when their people turned on their televisions or listened to their car radios or read their newspapers, Safeway was there and being talked about in a positive way or mentioned in a positive context. So, aside from the specific merger coverage, they carried on doing exactly what they would have done in normal circumstances in terms of launching new product ranges, big headline-grabbing promotions and so on. They also kept their name in the news, both on consumer-facing or industry-related issues. In fact, Safeway won the PR Week award for In-house Team of the Year for their efforts, which they submitted under the title "Alive and Kicking". And that was not the only national award Safeway won during the year.

(Information provided by Kevin Hawkins, Communications Director of Safeway until April 2004, Director General of the BRC until January 2008)

Keeping in touch with key talent

One multinational regularly surveyed people perceived as being key talent, whom the merged company would not want to lose. During the period between announcement and Day One a select sample of people were invited to lunch with the merger taskforce. They focused on the key talent, even though these bright scientists were often very outspoken and said things that were not always comfortable for senior managers to hear.

DEVELOPING THE RIGHT COMMUNICATION SKILLS FOR THE INTEGRATION

Even when it is not known exactly what sort of integration will be needed or who will be doing which jobs, some far-sighted organisations train managers in anticipation. This process recognises the intense importance of day-to-day communication from managers, outside of any formal communication process. The way managers answer daily questions and deal with the thousands of tiny changes needed in the new organisation will affect attitudes towards the new organisation at least as much as formal communication. As a responsible communication manager you need to be doing what you can to ensure that managers at all levels are equipped with the relevant skills.

Using the waiting time fruitfully

At Aviva managers were trained in the period between the announcement and the actual merger. During the training, managers:

- learned about the change curve and the timing of people's reactions;

- discussed the principles of the formation of the new organisation;

- focused on issues such as the plan for their business unit and how they were going to cope with the change at the same time as maintaining high standards in business as usual.

As we have seen, Safeway spent some of the long wait between announcement and Day One in training managers with the necessary skills in leadership. Waitrose, which bought 19 of the Safeway stores that the Competition Commission would not allow to go to Morrisons, also prepared the relevant managers with the relevant communication skills.

Checklist: Training for Line Managers

Line managers should receive training on the psychological impact and pattern of change, so that they are able to understand what happens to them and to their staff through the period of change. This training can include:

- Material on the *change curve*. Managers need to understand how people's reactions to announcements will differ depending on where they are in their personal change curve. The main lessons managers need to get from this training are that it is natural to have different emotional reactions at different stages and that they, as managers, may be ahead of the rest of their teams on the change curve. They therefore need to adjust their communication to be sensitive to their team's needs and refrain from getting impatient when people are still in an earlier stage than them.

- Understanding of how different *psychological types* view change and what sort of communication will be necessary for which sorts of people. It is useful to give managers a language to imagine how different some of their people may be from them. Any of the main personality or type indicators can be used. Ones that distinguish between people's behaviour in good times and under stress, such as LIFO or the Strengths Deployment Inventory, can be particularly helpful. The main purpose is to help managers think through the impact of change and announcements through a number of different eyes, so that they realise that other people may be different from them without being wrong.

- Specific skills for *listening to people*, such as feeding back to the individual what you have heard them say; not interrupting them; and listening for emotion and what is not being said as well as the actual words used.

Apart from anything else it gives management confidence to know that they are not only being equipped to communicate in the next few months but that their general skills base is being added to.

Building skills during the waiting period

In the old Inner London Education Authority (ILEA), after its closure was announced, the management introduced team briefings to run in the few months of existence it still had. This had various advantages:

- The training for managers gave them a transferable skill for their next jobs, whatever they might be.
- People felt that they were being cared about and invested in.
- It was imperative that the business of the Authority continued with high quality even as, with powers gradually being divested to the London Boroughs, people were leaving and processes were constantly changing. Team briefing gave local managers the opportunity to keep people up to date with what relevant work was being done where and to enthuse them about the work they were doing as a team, which remained viably important.
- It gave the organisation a method of listening to teams systematically as information was collected every month.

PLANNING THE COMMUNICATION INFRASTRUCTURE FOR THE NEW ORGANISATION

In cases where the merging organisations are competitors in a highly regulated market, it may not be possible to work at all across the two organisations in advance of Day One. In other cases, especially in the public sector, there may be no problems in working together as soon as the merger is announced. Or it may be possible to start working together at some stage in between the two dates, as the Regulator makes some key decisions, even if others are still awaited.

> The Competition Commission is an independent public body established by the Competition Act 1998. It replaced the Monopolies and Mergers Commission on 1 April 1999.
>
> The Commission conducts in-depth inquiries into mergers, markets and the regulation of the major regulated industries. Every inquiry is undertaken in response to a reference made to it by another authority: usually by the Office of Fair Trading (OFT) but in certain circumstances by the Secretary of State, or by the regulators under sector-specific legislative provisions relating to regulated industries. The Commission has no power to conduct inquiries on its own initiative.

The following are guidelines for internal communicators whenever it becomes possible for you to contact your opposite number.

- Providing contact is allowed between the organisations there is no need to wait until someone asks you to set up a working group.

- Check with your manager that you can take the initiative.

- Organise a meeting initially with your opposite number and then of your two teams.

- Some companies have found it helpful to have a facilitator for the first meeting.

- The agenda for first meeting should include:

  - sharing information about numbers and nature of work in the organisations, including such indicators as length of service of different categories of employee, age profile and so on;

  - sharing of information about how communication works in both organisations, being frank about what is successful and what is not;

  - giving some indications of the culture of both organisations;

  - communication teams, how they allocate work and who their closest relationships are with;

  - teambuilding activities;

  - building dialogue skills and other skills to help the team communicate with each other across the organisations.

Building an internal communications team across the organisations

Scottish Water was formed by a merger of three Scottish Water authorities into one. One of the internal communication managers identified the people responsible for internal communication across the three companies. She went to visit the relevant senior managers to get permission to release these people for a series of awaydays to work on communication for the new company.

The first awaydays were mainly teambuilding but included some visioning. The teambuilding was essential for engendering a positive attitude towards the changes that were needed. Among the exercises that were used to build this team was one called "I agree, I disagree" which built dialogue skills. People were given a scenario – getting a flying sausage to market – and had to present how they would do it. The purpose of the exercise was to make people give reasons for their views. This really taught people how to listen and also how to have a debate in a non-contentious way. It was an important achievement that, quite quickly, the team had moved away from an automatic reaction of "that would never work in — " to working together to think up solutions.

They then did a mini audit of communication and culture in the three organisations, channels, roles and means of measuring. The team was under intense time pressure and so had to work fast. The need to work together simply to get the work done also helped build the team, as did strong and confident leadership. The people in the team were all passionate about what they did.

It also helped that there was a strong structure in the way the internal communication manager ran the meetings. Every meeting always ended with everyone saying one thing they liked and one they did not about the meeting. It was very open and people were able to say when they had felt hurt by something someone had said. This meant that there was no bitterness that people took home with them.

Another useful factor was that the convenor of the meeting herself did not know initially whether or not she would keep her job. She was clear from the beginning that none of them knew if they would have jobs in the new organisation but that in the meantime it could do them nothing but good to do a superb job of the communication during the merger period. Either they would get jobs in the new organisation or the quality of the work they had done would stand them in good stead when looking for work elsewhere.

One of the pieces of work that the team did was to agree some principles of communication which would be used in the new organisation. One of these was that there should always be a name so that people knew who to go to for further information if they need it. Another principle was that there should be high levels of consultation. They also devised a strategy for each channel that they planned to use.

You may or may not be able to work closely with your opposite number at this stage. This will mainly depend on the regulatory process: if the proposed partner is a direct competitor you will not be allowed to share detailed information before the actual date of the merger.

Using a "clean team"

In Pfizer's acquisition of Pharmacia, there was a "clean team" who were not officers of either company, but were, for instance, recent retirees with great knowledge, who collected information. Because of regulatory requirements it was not possible for current officers to share information, but the clean team gathered information from both organisations so that it was ready for the moment when they were allowed to.

COMMUNICATION ABOUT THE OTHER PART OF THE ORGANISATION BEFORE DAY ONE

There will be immense curiosity about the other part of the organisation before Day One, with people googling them, studying their website, especially the career site, and looking for references in the press. Some are also likely to use social media sites, such as Facebook (for younger people), Linked In (for more established professionals) or industry specific chat rooms. The whole explosion of social media has made it impossible to disguise the nature of the employee experience, and employees are now likely to have a view of the other part of the organisation before Day One.

The more you can agree about tone of voice and vocabulary with your opposite numbers the better. This can be difficult if the parties have very different styles. Any differences will be particularly obvious if you do start to have some common material, whether in the form of publications or websites.

Using information in the public domain

Even if it is not possible to communicate across the organisations because of regulatory limitations, there is plenty of information in the public domain which can be presented to employees. In GlaxoWellcome and SmithKline Beecham there was a long wait while regulators pondered. The two organisations were limited in the information they were able to share with each other, but they did succeed in sharing identical information simultaneously through each company's established communications channels and having a joint merger publication, giving information about both companies, setting out a timeline for the process and, on the intranet, giving information as quickly as possible.

The *Emerge* publication was sent out between the announcement of the intention to merge and Day One, setting out the stages of a merger and giving information about the two organisations and about the senior people whose provisional appointments had already been announced.

PREPARATION FOR THE ANNOUNCEMENTS FOR DAY ONE

The more you can say on Day One the better. People will be thirsty for real news, and while generalisations about the strategy are perfectly appropriate for the initial announcement of the deal, by the day of the merger itself people will want real news about future structure and jobs.

This means that there is considerable work to be done in the two organisations in the weeks leading up to the actual merger. In most cases there are regulatory considerations which make it difficult for the two organisations to completely share information and planning before the day of the merger itself, but some planning together is usually possible.

In many cases the teams from the two organisations are only allowed to work together for a couple of weeks before Day One, in which time all the materials and logistics for Day One need to be prepared. If you cannot even talk to your opposite numbers, there is every danger that you will duplicate effort. This is better than neither of you doing the work, and if you really cannot speak with them, then you are better preparing for communication in both organisations than making assumptions about the competence or resources in the new partner.

Both the tone and media used for Day One communication will carry great weight. In some cases organisations have chosen a deliberately low profile for Day One, and have made no fuss at all. This might be particularly where the organisation knows it has not yet made any of the major decisions which people are awaiting. In most cases, however, a degree of impact is needed simply to reflect the fact that the public face of the organisation is changing. At the very least there is likely to be new stationery and possibly new signage.

With a view to keeping people's minds on the business, companies often underplay the extent of likely change on Day One. In our experience this is a mistake. Now is the moment when people are likely to be ready to hear about real change and they can feel betrayed later if there are unexpected uncomfortable changes.

Checklist: Decisions to Communicate on or Around Day One

Here is a checklist for the decisions that you might communicate on Day One. You will not always have this information, but this would be the ideal:

- The composition of the top team, including something about their personal backgrounds and priorities: each member of the top team should be ready to make personal statements to the people who will be working for them in the new entity.

- The selection process by which these people were chosen: employees will scrutinise the list carefully, hoping to decode from the balance of jobs going to people from each of the former companies who will be the winners in the new entity.

- The new structure for the top layer or two.

- Some sort of statement about the degree of integration anticipated and the extent to which the target will be left alone.

- A plan for the first 100 days, or at least an announcement of what the workstreams are going to be, who is on them and what their terms of reference are.

- The process whereby people are to be selected, at least for the next layer down of jobs if not more.

- A statement about future harmonisation of terms and conditions of employment and pension arrangements: while these are usually protected initially under TUPE, people will be keen to know what the longer-term plans are.

- Some reference to the character or personality of the new organisation, for example, the extent to which it will be centralised, how it plans to deal with its key stakeholders including employees. It is usually too early to talk about values unless the deal is a clear acquisition where the target will be expected to work within the bidder's values, but it is possible to add some personality to the bald strategy.

- A reiteration of the rationale for the deal with more detail about the strategy if it is available. You may think you have communicated the rationale for the deal to death but some people will still not have taken it in and will only start to when decisions closer to them start to emerge. The people working on the deal, especially those responsible for communication, can probably recite the rationale in their sleep, but it will not have had the same brain time for others in the organisation, whose focus is on other matters. One of the most common mistakes we see in merger communication is the failure to keep hammering home the rationale.

Decisions about the Degree of Integration

One of the roles of the communicator is to inject a note of realism into discussions about the extent of integration planned. In our experience, organisations often plan to have very little integration and often communicate this fact at the time of the merger itself or sometimes even at the time of the announcement. In practice there is often, over the next months or years, a creeping integration, which is much resented and causes a degree of distrust of the new management.

It seems that pressures on organisations in the twenty-first century are such that it is difficult to sustain an organisation managed at arm's length. Although we have seen it done successfully where the target has a clearly differentiated product or market segment, in most cases the acquired organisation is eventually fully integrated, often after a hiccough with results, a public relations crisis or the need for cost-cutting resulting in elimination of duplication and inconsistencies.

There are two main reasons why organisations tend towards integration whatever the initial intentions:

1. The need to protect the corporate reputation. This can play over the full range of corporate social responsibility, with the Group wanting to make demands on the subsidiaries over a wide range of matters. On the people front this can extend to its employment reputation, over such things as employee relations

and employment tribunals, which lead to interference in the way the acquired company carries out its detailed and day-to-day management. Alternatively, the parent may be keen to have a squeaky clean image for transparent executive remuneration and therefore not be willing to let the subsidiary decide its own bonus or other reward strategy. In other cases the Group may feel that its reputation is tied up with that of its chief executive and it will demand that there are no other stars emerging.

2.   Once the figures go wrong there is a loss of nerve in the centre and the subsidiary is given less freedom to run things its own way.

What Needs to be Prepared for Day One

A plan for communication to all the various stakeholders inside and outside the organisation

Although the core message might be the same for all audiences – the rationale for the deal and what the hope is for the new organisation in broad terms – the details and media to be used will need to be planned separately for each audience. In many cases the communicators for the three sets of audiences – the public, the City/shareholders and employees – work together to plan the announcements, aware that the audiences overlap.

Preparation usually includes the agreement of a form of words and a tone of voice that will be consistent across the stakeholder groups.

A set of scripts for employees for their conversations with external stakeholders

A wide range of employees deal with suppliers and customers. It is essential that they are confident about what to say to these external groups. This is particularly true where employees have personal relationships with customers, for example where the customers may trust their contact rather than formal communication from the organisation. It is essential that the messages from their trusted contact and the formal ones from the organisation do not contradict each other in tone or content. It is helpful to give people scripts for the conversations and to encourage them to be proactive about having the conversations, rather than waiting for the customer or supplier to contact them. It can also be helpful to give them Q&As that anticipate the most common questions.

Materials

It is useful to be able to give everyone some materials on Day One. These usually include:

*   Some sort of brochure or leaflet about the new company, introducing the top team, locations, products and customers. If the new identity has been agreed the brochure should explain the rationale for it. This

brochure should also set out a timeline for the next announcements
and any integration dates that are known.

- Some sort of tangible object with the new identity such as a mug,
  T-shirt or mouse mat.

Materials for Day One: TUI Travel Mainstream

The brochure TUI Travel Mainstream sent to all their new employees on Day One
of the merger of First Choice and Thomson in September 2007 had:

- a message from the MD;

- a page on the history of the two companies;

- a top-level organisation chart with some basic facts and figures about the
  number of employees, locations, and so on;

- profiles of the leadership team;

- the timetable for integration;

- questions page.

In addition to this at Group level there were webcasts on Day One and a
combined intranet side called TUItogether.com.

Some sort of joint website should be available from Day One, even though
most material will not of course yet be migrated from the old intranets, but
do not think this can substitute for a written document. People will want to
take something home to show family and friends.

Materials for Day One: GSK

When GlaxoWellcome merged with SmithKline Beecham they were able on Day
One to deliver the following to people's desks, so that they were there when they
arrived for work:

- "Spirit of GSK" brochure (outlining the culture framework for the new company,
  including mission, strategic intent, business drivers, a credo and core values);

- heritage brochure;

- information about the corporate brand;

- their new security pass (the photos having been taken in advance).

They had managed to keep the new corporate identity under wraps and so were
able to have maximum impact on Day One. There were Brand Champions in
each of the countries who managed the practicalities of getting printing, and so
on, done, and there were strict design guidelines.

On this day they were able to coordinate:

- unveiling of the new GSK brand identity;

- a global satellite broadcast;

- press advertising;

- a CEO Home Page on the intranet;

- a GSK intranet/internet (internal 'global news' service);

- a launch video.

Face-to-face or satellite meetings

Where possible face-to-face meetings should be held, involving senior people.
In a multi-site operation this requires different managers to go to different
places and/or satellite meetings. A low-tech equivalent, using just a telephone
conferencing facility backed up by local management, is better than nothing.

The content of the meetings should be similar to that of the brochures,
with as much content as possible about an exciting vision of how the new
company might be. Even at this stage the rationale for the deal needs to be
repeated, but what people are really looking for on Day One is a sense of
excitement that they are working for an organisation that has a clear and
inspiring view of where it is trying to get to and a competent management
team who can lead it there. Emphasis should be placed on the new company's
place in the context of its market and competitors, talking about the
challenges of anticipated change. People should leave these meetings excited
about the new organisation and confident in its success.

As with the brochure, the other main topic for the meetings is the timetable
and process for the next stages. Of course you do not have an answer
today for the questions people care most about ("Have I still got a job?" for
example); but you can at least tell them as much as you know about the
process for making that sort of decision and an outline timetable. If possible
tell them, too, how they can get involved, whether through unions or
employee representatives or more directly by contributing to chat rooms or
local meetings organised by workstreams.

Communicating with distant, small site or home-workers

With email being pretty much universal among office workers there is
often a view that the problem of instantaneous communication has been
solved. Yet there are still millions of employees not covered by email, whose
communication needs on Day One need to be planned for and met, such as
those working in retail or in factories, drivers, outdoor workers, and so on.

The brochures may need to be mailed to home addresses and it is important
that some face-to-face meetings with at least reasonably senior people are
made available to people at a location near to them within the first few
weeks. If the merger or acquisition is likely to have a big impact on the site

it is worth equipping local managers with a full briefing kit a little like that outlined for the announcement in Chapter 3.

CONSULTATION – TUPE AND OTHERWISE

The regulations concerning the consultation of employees in the event of a transfer of undertakings are extremely complicated and are constantly being amended or clarified. It is important that you know where you stand in terms of TUPE: whether your deal means that people are doing TUPE transfers and, if they are, what their rights are in terms of consultation. In broad terms employees in a TUPE transfer are entitled to have their elected representatives consulted in advance of a transfer. Your lawyers will be able to brief you on the relevant facts for your merger or acquisition.

Whether or not your transfer is covered by the legislation there are obvious advantages in consulting fully at this stage, as at every other where major decisions are being made. Close and trusting relations with unions or other employee representatives will pay dividends when difficult decisions must be negotiated and disseminated.

KEY PLAYERS

Following the announcement of the deal a much wider range of people are involved. The most important people for you to be working with at this stage are:

- HR, who will be starting to make decisions about appointments or at least about the process for deciding appointments. They will also be dealing with TUPE and the unions.

- Communication colleagues working with other audiences who will also be preparing for Day One.

- The integration team or chief if one has been appointed. This is a particularly important relationship for you as they will need to be listening and disseminating information throughout, and you need to establish a mutually beneficial way of working with them from the outset.

WHAT SORT OF LISTENING TO DO AT THIS STAGE

Now is not the moment for high-profile surveys. However, it is important to keep your ear to the ground to find out what rumours are circulating. Even if you do not know the answers yet it can be helpful just to acknowledge people's concerns so that they know you are listening.

It is particularly important to listen to managers to find out their confidence levels with the communication and management challenges they are likely to face. This can help design the training to meet the most pressing needs.

It is also essential that there are channels for individual questions, even though, again, the answers may be in short supply. A top question will be about pensions and it is important that there are telephone numbers or intranet site addresses published where people can direct their queries. Even if the answer is "We don't know yet", it is helpful to hear that authoritatively, rather than be prey to the gloomy rumours going around the office.

Other likely topics will be redundancy terms and the implications of TUPE. Again, it is important to give correct information as far as it is known. You will probably need to work closely with your HR colleagues to ensure that people are given facts not guesswork. Incorrect information or uncontrolled rumours at this stage will poison future communication and possibly the future relationship with your acquired employees.

Listening between announcement and Day One

Pfizer ran regular "pulse sessions" from the time of the announcement of the acquisition of Pharmacia. There was a group of representatives from the support functions which met weekly for an hour, asking "What have you picked up?", "What are their concerns?" This was used to feed in to communication on an ongoing basis.

WHAT EMPLOYEES ARE THINKING AND SAYING

What You Want Them to be Thinking and Saying

I hope the deal goes ahead. It sounds like an excellent organisation.

I still want to know what's going to happen to this site, but at least I'm confident I'll hear as soon as a decision is made.

We don't know much about this yet, but at least our management care about keeping us informed.

What You Don't Want Them to be Thinking and Saying

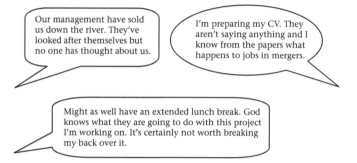

THE COST OF GETTING IT WRONG

• A poor tone at the outset will take a lot of living down.

• Missing out audiences or appearing to give them second-class treatment in the announcements may stir up lasting resentment.

• Failing to create a relationship with your opposite number when you can may result in inconsistencies in the story being told in the two organisations.

• Failing to equip managers with the necessary skills may make you vulnerable when the detailed announcements need to be made.

• If the grapevine starts telling too gloomy a view it may be difficult to raise impressions later, whatever the news.

SUMMARY FOR INTERNAL COMMUNICATORS

1. This is bound to be a frustrating time, when everyone wants answers which you do not have. All you can do is communicate that you understand what their questions are and that you share their frustration.

2. If there is a protracted period between the announcement and Day One you can use this time for preparation, both in developing communication skills for integration and, if you are able to work with your opposite number, in planning the communication infrastructure for the new organisation.

3. There will be a great deal of logistical planning for Day One as well, which is likely to occupy much of your time.

4. You need to monitor communication about the other organisation and ensure that you are communicating about them too, although you will almost certainly be limited to material that is in the public domain.

5 Stage Five: The First 100 Days

IMPORTANCE OF THE FIRST 100 DAYS

As we have seen, the announcement and Day One are important in setting the tone for the new organisation, but the first 100 days are even more important. People will realise that the announcement and Day One have been stage-managed to give a certain impression. They will be watching carefully in the first 100 days to see what the new organisation is really going to be like.

There is also a unique opportunity in the first 100 days. There is a small window at the beginning of a new organisation when people will expect change and be ready for it. This opportunity should not be wasted. We are often called into organisations six months or a year after a merger, when there is both resistance to change and the emergence of a strong them-and-us mentality. This has often been exacerbated by the organisation saying in the first days of the new organisation that they did not intend to change much and that the important thing was maintaining business as usual. People were lulled into thinking that things would not change and were therefore not expecting it. In contrast, where the change is visible from the first day there is a different mindset.

One of the opportunities of the first 100 days is for some quick wins. It can have a major impact just to solve some of the ongoing gripes, such as fixing a leaky roof, replacing one or two pieces of poor equipment which blight employees' lives or even just redecorating. Highly visible improvements have an immediate impact which shapes the way employees interpret the other changes they see over the first few months. It also helps set the tone to under-promise and over-deliver; employees will get the impression that the new management team is competent.

It is worth emphasising some of the more visible changes. We have already mentioned signage in Chapter 4. Over the first 100 days you need to make sure that images throughout the new organisation represent it and not the old one.

> **Getting the visual communication right**
>
> One of the things Colin Archer did as internal communication manager in
> Centrica Energy Management was to make sure that the pictures in the reception
> areas, corridors and meeting rooms of newly acquired sites showed Centrica sites
> and not those of the former owners.

Of course it is hard to concentrate on setting the tone for the new
organisation when the key players are so busy with immediate business:
making arrangements with major suppliers and customers, dealing with the
top people issues and continuing long hours with advisers all absorb time and
attention. Very often people are exhausted from making the deal itself and
getting to Day One.

There is often a view among top managers that, hard as things are for people
to begin with, they will soon "settle down". Our experience suggests that
they do not. Poor relations established in the first 100 days just deteriorate
until something positive is done to mend them; and the longer they are left,
the harder it is to recover them. One of your first tasks as communicator,
therefore, is to stress the importance of these first 100 days to the top
management and to give them clear guidance about what they should be
doing at this time in communication terms.

Many of the changes people face in the first days of a merger are exactly the
same as in any other major change programme: volume of new information,
bad news for some and worry while waiting for major decisions. The
differences are that in this case there is often a visible and easy "enemy" in
the form of the other company, and in addition there is the challenge of
communicating using two different established communication methods in
the different organisations.

Different Degrees of Integration and the Implications at this Stage

The communication challenges of the first 100 days vary according to the
degree of integration that the organisation is planning. This in turn depends
on the aims of the deal. If it is to eliminate overcapacity or any other cost-
cutting reason, it is likely that a fair degree of integration will be sought,
at least in parts of the organisation, typically back-office or supply-chain
functions. In this case change will strike both parts of the new organisation.

Other aims will have uneven impact on the organisations, depending on the
detail. If the aim of the deal was geographical, product or market extension
it is possible that both parts will be largely left alone, except for some specific
integration in the finance areas and other departments affected. In other
deals, where a particular perceived gap in the parent company has been met

by acquisition, the smaller function in the buyer company, now superseded by the acquisition, may be the more affected.

COMMUNICATION ISSUES FOR THE FIRST 100 DAYS

Because of its unique opportunities as well as its unique dangers, communication in the first 100 days has a range of challenges which, while they are always there for communicators, are particularly important to meet at this time. They are:

- managing the dilemma between speed and the need to consult;

- dealing with the communication "vacuum" when there is no news;

- communicating when there is a danger of low trust and credibility;

- supporting new leaders;

- dealing with change and the resistance to change;

- avoiding overload of communication whereby people are inundated with messages but cannot see a clear picture;

- communicating redundancy, which is often a major issue in the first 100 days;

- communicating business as usual when you and managers throughout the organisation are distracted with integration issues.

We will look in more detail at each of these issues in turn.

Importance of Speed versus the Need to Consult

Lawrence J. Demonaco, Senior Vice President of Human Resources at GE Capital, talked to 25 CEOs of companies they had acquired and asked them to identify one thing that they should have done differently. All but one of the CEOs said they should have moved faster on integration (Light 2001).

People need to be put out of their misery quickly and the organisation needs to be able to put the pain of transition behind it as soon as possible so that it can get on with the business of building a new organisation. On the other hand, change writers often stress the need to build a change coalition and to involve as many people as possible in making the decisions. Unfortunately, you can't have both.

Communicators are often in a sort of push-me-pull-you position where they have to make difficult decisions between the two approaches.

To complicate the matter further there are also legal obligations to consult employees or their representatives. These apply in three separate situations, all of which are often present during a merger or acquisition: the transfer of undertakings, collective redundancies and, in certain circumstances, any change affecting "the recent and probable developments of the undertaking's activities and economic situation", including specifically the numbers or nature of employment. The gist of these myriad regulations is that employees or their representatives need to be consulted in good time before changes affecting them are made, and can claim compensation if the consultation in not genuine or timely. The more consultation that can be done in advance of Day One, the more easily these requirements can be met.

Advantages of speedy decision-making

- People can concentrate on business as usual as soon as possible.

- Psychological trauma is not drawn out.

- If you make choices on management structures and roles quickly, decisions can be made by the people who will have to make them work.

- Less politics: internal battles are not allowed to continue while decisions are still in abeyance.

- Shows strong and decisive leadership.

- Minimises the personal stress on individuals in a time of uncertainty.

- The longer the period of uncertainty lasts, the longer people will waste time in gossip and whingeing. Carbrera (1986) says people can lose up to two hours per day gossiping.

Advantages of wide consultation in advance of decision-making

- Decisions are more likely to be right since they will be made in the light of more knowledge and expertise.

- People are more committed to change they have helped design.

- You can get reaction of learned helplessness if change is too fast, so that when you do need people to contribute ideas again, they may have lost the inclination or energy to do so.

- Being actively involved in the process of designing the new organisation can itself be motivating and encourage people to consider staying rather than leaving.

- Unilateral decisions by the acquirer will send a message that employees in the target are not valued.

- The flip side of strong and decisive leadership is that it can seem out of touch and inflexible.

- Consultation is required by law under the Transfer of Undertakings Regulations and the Information and Consultation Directive.

- Involving managers and other key people in the consultation process gives you a chance to evaluate them in action, rather than having to rely on previous appraisals or selection tests.

The worst of both worlds is to delay decision-making to consult and then fail to take into account what people have said. If you do consult it is important to say, when the decision is finally taken, how it has been influenced by employee views. If the decision is against the flow of opinions you need to explain why the particular representations were unsuccessful.

The term "consultation" is a broad one. As well as the formal bodies necessary to meet legal requirements, consultation can and should include a range of informal methods through focus groups, working groups or even ordinary team meetings as well as that involving formal bodies. It can also include online methods such as opportunities to contribute to a wiki or chat room. The range of informal methods of consultation will be particularly important during the implementation phase, when detail and practicalities need to be established.

The varying needs of different employee groups will be discussed later in this chapter.

Table 5.1   Speed versus consultation

When best to go for speed	When best to go for consultation
You are likely to be losing a lot of people in a particular area or site.	
You want to make a new psychological contract.	You do not want to break the current psychological contract, for example, when it is essential that you keep an existing workforce.
Commercial pressures mean that the new organisation needs to be operating quickly.	Commercial pressures indicate that getting changes right will be more important than getting them implemented quickly.
Where there is low trust people may not trust the process or believe that their interventions have made a difference. In this case it might be best to go for quick decision-making and start to build the trust after the first 100 days.	Where people are accustomed to being consulted and there are well-established channels for consultation, they may feel particularly affronted if decisions are made without consultation. Any abrupt change of management style is likely to lead to lower morale.
Where there is no history of consultation people may well view such an exercise with suspicion. Any abrupt change of management style is likely to lead to lower morale.	Even if you have decided not to consult on the decision itself it can be helpful to consult on the implementation.

105

Dealing with the Communication Vacuum

However much you decide to opt for speed, there will be many cases when you simply cannot make important decisions quickly enough, for example because they are dependent on bigger decisions. Dealing with the communication vacuum when you have nothing to say is one of the hardest challenges of the first 100 days. Inevitably, there will be occasions when people will be crying out for information that is simply not yet available. This waiting on decisions is inevitably painful for people, partly because it prevents them from getting on with the rest of their lives. There is tension for them as other decisions that they need to take, such as moving home or choosing schools for their children, have to be postponed. Figure 5.1 illustrates the different types of communication appropriate for information of varying degrees of importance and certainty.

It is also a hard time for people because the lack of decisions makes them feel powerless.

What can you do to help?

- It is worth communicating frankly that you understand the frustration people are feeling.

- Make sure that people are aware that someone in charge knows who is waiting for what decisions, and that they will be told as soon as there is any movement.

- Keep listening to the concerns even if you have nothing to add. Don't stop the questions coming in just because you have no answers.

- Communicate as much about the process and timing of decision-making as you can. People's misery is increased if they believe rumours that decisions have already been taken but for some reason

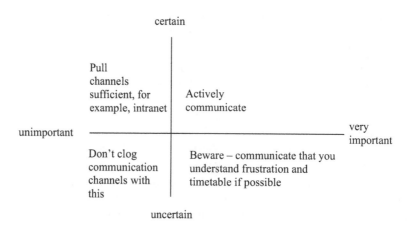

Figure 5.1   Importance/certainty grid

not yet announced. The more information people have about the structure of decision-making the better, so that they know the actual meeting at which the decision will be taken and who will be present. Decisions from the meeting can then be posted quickly on the intranet, and email alerts sent to those requesting them.

- Make sure that the leaders of the business are seen and don't become invisible. They will be inclined not to expose themselves to Q&A sessions at this stage because they know they do not have the answers, but it is still important that they are seen to be around and communicating, even if it is wiser to have walkabouts and announcements rather than requesting questions where there are no answers.

- Make sure that you have the communication infrastructure in place so that decisions can be communicated quickly and questions answered once the announcement is ready. Once you have earned a reputation for quick and accurate communication of decisions, people will develop confidence that they will not be kept in the dark any longer than necessary.

Checklist: Helping people overcome the feeling of helplessness

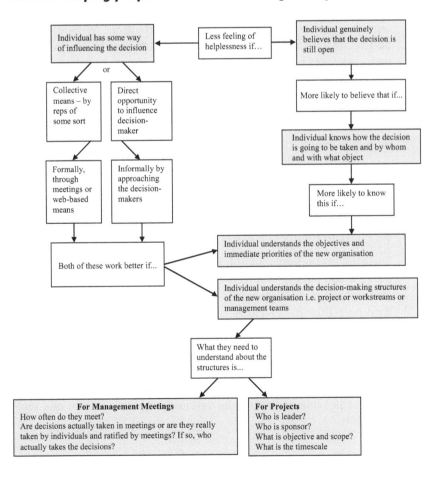

Credibility and Trust

As we have already seen from the Introduction, trust among leaders generally is at a low ebb in the early twenty-first century. For various reasons they are particularly under threat during a merger. In the first place, public reporting of mergers is often associated with job cuts; and secondly, employees perceive that the old management, in whom they may have had more or less trust, may themselves lose power during the merger, to be replaced by unknown people with unknown motivation.

If trust is low, communication is not believed; and if our communication is not believed, there is little point in doing it. The establishment of credibility and trust must therefore be essential parts of the communicator's job.

What makes a piece of information credible?

There are a number of factors that make a piece of information more likely to be believed.

> *It is frequently repeated and it comes from a number of sources.* With the range of channels open to an internal communicator this does not pose a practical challenge; the problem is the danger of overload. At first sight one might think the solution simple: not to repeat information but make sure it is correctly targeted the first time. While this might be true for operational information on which people need to act, the main messages need to be repeated through the various channels. The key message is the rationale for the deal. There will obviously be other important messages as changes are announced, but the rationale needs to be repeated, as otherwise it can be forgotten in the welter of new information. Whenever people encounter inconvenience they need to be able to remind themselves of the reasons for the deal.

> *It is consistent with other sources.* The Conference Board alleges that people are more likely to believe information that has not been targeted at them. Thus, employees are more likely to believe what they read in national or local papers and journalists are more likely to believe what they have heard from employees.

> The implication for communicators is that you need to be as careful in the first 100 days as you have been earlier to work with your external communication colleagues, as well as with the communication team in the other half of the new entity. However crude the formal communication systems between the two sides of the new company, you can rely on grapevines working well; one half of the company saying something inconsistent with what the other half is saying will soon be discerned.

> It also means that you need to be careful to control communication as far as possible, including the various integration groups and senior managers.

It is consistent with what they know to be true. Employees are a much more knowing audience than many external ones. They simply will not buy messages which are inconsistent with what they see around them. This applies in particular to claims about the new culture, but also to practical information about service levels or progress. Sometimes managers, in an effort to impress new senior managers, claim progress somewhat prematurely or optimistically. If this happens, and communication reaches employees which they know to be untrue, it damages the credibility of all the other information, too. As communicators you need to check facts before publishing, until you are confident of the accuracy of an internal source.

Claims about culture or values often lack credibility at this stage. Where a much larger organisation has taken over a smaller one, and the acquirer is confident of its culture and values, there is a chance of credibility. Where the merger or acquisition has parties more equal in size neither party's former values are likely to apply to the whole organisation and you should be wary of claiming any. The proclaimed values which are most likely to be ridiculed are those alleging care for employees at a time when so many are feeling unsure of their future. The former organisation's values are, anyway, likely to be thrown in your face.

Building trust can take time

Centrica bought a power station in 2003. It had formerly been owned by a US company which had put a great deal of effort into communicating a set of values, including "integrity". They had then mothballed the plant prior to its purchase by Centrica. The employees kept referring to "integrity" and the new employer undeservedly inherited some cynicism. It took some time with Centrica giving regular and reliable communication before employees started to trust them.

It is presented in a two-sided way. This point is particularly important in the first 100 days, as people will be wary of "spin" or bias in communication at this time. Presenting a decision by talking about the main alternatives and their advantages as well as the chosen one shows you have listened to employees' views and given credit to their intelligence. It also helps disarm some negative rumours as it shows you have listened to the contrary points of view and have reasons for the decisions you have taken.

It is presented by someone attractive. This is a research finding which is worth bearing in mind when considering speakers for employee events. You may find yourself having to advise on grooming as well as the communication skills of projection.

It comes from a source which has proved reliable in the past. This can prove a problem if one party to the deal has been using channels which have fallen into disrepute as a result of unreliability in the past.

There is also a problem if employees have learned not to believe their management. In such a case it will take time before they will start to believe communications, even if they come from a completely new management team. If a channel has lost credibility, the best thing is to close it down. If it is a useful sort of channel it can be re-opened later, under a different name and with some different characteristics, and it can then have a chance to build credibility up from scratch.

Surveys conducted during the due diligence phase should tell you which channels are believed for which sort of information, so you know what will work.

It accords with what people expect. Rita Cruise O'Brien (2001) has shown that trust depends on both cognitive and affective judgement. The cognitive judgement is an assessment of reliability, competence, fairness and consistency, while the affective judgement is faith in care, concern, openness and support. In her 1995 study of organisations following mergers she found that only 9 per cent of top managers had a sincere interest in the welfare of employees, and, fittingly, only 8 per cent of employees believed that management could be counted on to give a fair deal. Recent research from Roffey Park (2007) suggests that a slightly higher figure, but still only 24 per cent of employees, trust senior managers to a great extent.

This lack of trust presents a huge challenge to internal communicators. Trust can only be built gradually but can be lost in an instant with an ill-judged mismatch between words and actions. As Cruise O'Brien indicates it is also multi-dimensional and there are a range of attributes managers need to show over time in order to build trust.

Eight rules to build trust

1. Deliver what you say you will deliver. This can often be particularly important where employees have seen promises broken under a former regime, typically in a target organisation where performance was dropping. It will take more than the first 100 days to build up trust, but at least you can start by making announcements the day you say you will make them, and meeting deadlines for other changes. The key lesson here is not to promise anything in the first 100 days that you are not absolutely sure you can deliver.

2. Make sure that all communication is crystal clear and that there is no room for misunderstanding or misinterpretation. If statements are made in business jargon that is not understood by employees it cannot be the basis of building up trust, even if you achieve all your targets. It is worth testing complicated messages with a selection of their intended audiences. Where people fail to understand content they sometimes think that information has been deliberately obscured and then seek reasons for the concealment.

3.   Make sure that communication is consistent. This can be a real challenge when it is being delivered by many managers throughout the organisation.

**Make sure managers understand what
they are asked to communicate**

When feeding back results from an employee survey one organisation used mean scores, presented simply in bar chart form but with inadequate explanation. A junior manager, when confronted by employees who could not see their "strongly disagree" scores, agreed with them that the results were "all lies".

---

4.   Be assertive with top managers when you see them acting in ways that will damage trust. You need to point out if they are inconsistent, either between words and action or between different things they are saying, and remind them of the cost of low trust.

Communication principles

The following communication principles are from a specific integration project in EDF:

- be timely;

- tell staff what to do/what not to do;

- be clear and to the point;

- explain consequences;

- be targeted when possible;

- use suitable media;

- establish and use feedback channels;

- be in context;

- be balanced;

- be consistent across the branch;

- be accurate;

- be branded when necessary;

- be established early to promote familiarity;

- avoid information overload.

5. Agree some sensible principles for communication and get them agreed at a senior level. These should be thought through and if possible avoid the simplistic. A common principle is "Communication should be open and honest". This is undeliverable. Communication cannot be totally open. All communication is necessarily selective and there are many occasions when it would be unwise or in breach of Stock Exchange regulations to be open, for example early in the process of considering potentially explosive options or when price-sensitive or competitive information is involved. It is therefore not a simple matter of principle but a sensitive matter of judgement how open to be. The point is, however, that you should not be deliberately misleading or unnecessarily secretive.

6. In an endeavour to be open, communicators sometimes make the mistake of giving employees the same information as they give the City. While this information should be available to all it only succeeds in communicating to a small number of managers or accountants in most organisations. You need actively and regularly to communicate simpler performance information, concentrating on one or two key figures such as sales and profit. Now is not the time for a major exercise in business education; concentrate on a few key indicators and do not blind or confuse people with too much active communication on figures.

7. Research indicates that trust is in danger when there are too many initiatives at once. The first 100 days are usually awash with initiatives, some of them related to the merger or acquisition, others delivering continuous improvement. All you can do as a communicator is to show how they are all related, so that they seem to be aspects of one or two great initiatives rather than a plethora of unrelated ones.

8. There are also indications that people begin to trust management on the basis of consistent and frequent information about how the company is doing in such a way that they can understand.

In addition to the explicit messages you send, every tiny move and change can send implicit messages. Employees of both parts of the new organisation will be watching every move and interpreting every statement like kremlinologists.

In working alongside your HR colleagues, you need also to be looking out for mismatches between the overt messages in the formal communication and the actual messages sent out by the behaviour and processes of the organisation. Two of the most powerful messages are about who gets promoted and what the organisation pays highly for.

Who gets promoted?

This sends strong messages throughout the organisation about what its values really are. People will make interpretations based on the achievements or the attributes of the high-profile promotions within the company. If the company has had to go outside for most or all of its recent promotions that, too, tells its own tale. It says that the people in the organisation currently do not have the sort of talents that are needed for the future and that there is not much future for ambitious people within the organisation. Some of the more ambitious employees may already have left; others will be looking to go, or be looking to gain their satisfaction from sources outside their business life. Contradictory messages about valuing internal talent and wanting to develop people for their and the organisation's future benefit will be disbelieved.

Turning to internal appointments, people will be looking carefully to see the match between what is said publicly in terms of values and competencies, and the characteristics these people are seen to have. If, for example, blustering bullies or mavericks, who nevertheless made their figures, are seen to be promoted then the message people will get is that only the figures matter and behaviour to colleagues, teamwork, and so on, are irrelevant, in spite of what is explicitly stated and communicated.

Employees will also be watching for unfairness in selection, in particular for managers selecting their own cronies from the part of the organisation they came from. They will also be trying to interpret the future direction of the organisation from the known skills and experience of appointees, for example are they known for cost-cutting or for outsourcing?

The important things to communicate are the process, including the selection criteria and who makes selection decisions, the timetable for appointments and the way in which appointments will be announced.

Who gets paid what?

Of course nothing is more emotive than pay. Under TUPE regulations new employees automatically keep their terms and conditions and there may be inconsistencies between the two organisations about how highly valued different jobs are. However detailed the due diligence has been there are usually some nasty surprises when, after Day One, some of the details of terms and conditions are revealed. They can be a cause of jealousy and distrust whether or not you seek to harmonise. Employees will be on the look out for unfairness.

Difficulties of varying terms and conditions

One organisation we worked with was founded from the merger of three software companies. One had rewarded its people by allowing them to choose any car they wanted (within a certain value) as a company car. Men in their mid-twenties were driving around in Porshes and Ferraris. The other companies had more traditional car policies.

Relationships within the new organisation were damaged. The lucky ones were convinced that "unimaginative bureaucracy" of the new organisation would deprive them of their wheels, while others were furious that they were not going to have the same privileges.

Challenges of perceived unfairness: people only notice what is wrong

Another organisation we worked with bought a company with people doing identical work, where almost everything in the terms and conditions was different. At huge expense the acquirer brought everyone up to the higher level of the different terms – including holiday entitlement, bonuses, pay rates and pensions – in everything except the length of the working day. No one in focus groups mentioned the improvements, while the resentment over "them" having a shorter working day dominated attitudes.

This issue strikes employees at a number of different levels: which occupational groups or levels are particularly well paid compared to other organisations; and within any particular population what are people rewarded extra for. Both of these tell people what is really valued in the organisation. Your HR colleagues will be looking to see the pay policy's consistency with strategy and for any contractual horrors which it will take on. Your chief concern is its consistency with explicit messages.

The harm in having inconsistent messages in either promotions or pay is not merely to the credibility of the specific messages, often associated with espoused values, but to the whole of the communication from the organisation to its people. If you are trying to assess trust then looking for contradictions of this sort is a good way of assessing whether the organisation has built up deserved trust or actually dissipates it.

Values and Culture

Only rarely are organisations ready to announce the new values on or soon after Day One. GlaxoSmithKline managed to do this, with The GSK Way, a cultural framework agreed in advance by the new executive team. Normally work on values waits until the dust has settled. We do, however, suggest that some work is done enunciating some principles for the integration itself and that the integration project team or workstream members do some cultural awareness raising work as part of their early work together as a team. GSK also has a fine example of integration principles (see box).

GSK integration principles

- Respect the history, culture, people and processes of both companies.

- Adopt an objective, transparent and timely decision-making process.

- Identify and retain the people and practices best suited to running the business through an open, fair and impartial process.

- Communicate in an honest, open, timely and two-way manner as appropriate.

Supporting New Leaders

People will look for leadership in a time of uncertainty and the communicator must help the new leaders of the organisation meet this need.

The most important audience is the senior management, who need to feel valued and included. Some time within the first 100 days, preferably within the first 30, you need to organise a conference or meeting of the senior people in the organisation. Depending on the size and geographical spread of the organisation this may take considerable effort and time when senior people have so many other things on their plates. Employees understand this and senior management taking the time out to show visibility in the first 100 days will pay off in terms of long-term attitudes towards them.

Change and Resistance to Change

Managers often say that people hate change and automatically resist it. Our experience does not bear this out. People love change. Why else do they spend their leisure improving their houses, shopping for new things or looking for new experiences? How often, when you run a focus group for people about work, do they say, "Well, I wouldn't like to see any changes around here really; things are pretty much perfect"? Practically never. They almost always have a list of things they would like to see changed, whether it is the way their work is organised or the relationships around them.

It is, however, clear that employees often do resist change, especially in the aftermath of a merger or acquisition. The issue is therefore not that people oppose all change; it is that they oppose *some* change at work. Our experience suggests that there are two main reasons: either it is actually against their interests, or they lack confidence that they will thrive in a new job or environment. Table 5.2 looks at different reasons for resistance and what the communicator can do to minimise the resistance.

Table 5.2   Minimising employee resistance to change

Reason for resistance	Communicator's response
The proposed change is actually against their interests	
Sometimes it is obviously so: for example a change in hours or place of work to ones which are less convenient or which necessitate difficult adjustments in personal arrangements, or fewer opportunities to earn through allowances or overtime.	This is partly a matter for your HR colleagues, making sure that there is adequate recompense for a deterioration in terms and conditions, but you will also have your part to play, ensuring that there are the right channels in place to hear the exact concerns that people have and to communicate the advantages of the new arrangements to them (if there are any) and to the organisation.

Table 5.2   *Continued*

	If the changes are frankly a deterioration, it is particularly important to communicate why there was no alternative, with reference to the external context, for example, competition. A necessary element of the communication is simply accurate information about the proposed or new conditions. Rumours on these topics have particularly effective wings and you need to have quick ways of communicating and swift, reliable channels for dealing with questions.
Sometimes it is less obvious, and relates to ways that, over time, people manage to organise their working lives in a way that suits their personal interests. For example, all of us have aspects of our jobs which we dislike and/or are bad at. Over time we manage to avoid them. Either we persuade colleagues to take them on or we just stop doing them and after a while the boss gives up on nagging us into doing them. We may have found other ways of making our working lives pleasanter, by making sure we spend time with colleagues we like or organising our working space to be congenial. The social aspect of work is often overlooked but is important to people. Many people have their closest and deepest friendships with colleagues; they may well fear losing day-to-day contact with them. There may even be arrangements for working time which have never been formally enshrined in contracts, whereby they regularly work from home, or leave early, for the sake of something in their personal lives. People may fear (perhaps with good reason) that such custom and practice benefits may be lost when terms and conditions are changed.	This is harder territory for the communicator. These issues are largely individual although some may occur at team level. They are also often unsayable; people may not even be consciously aware of the reason why the proposed change seems unattractive. If they are aware that they have adjusted their jobs to suit them they may believe that there would be little sympathy for trying to keep the practices they have gradually introduced. All you can do here is to ensure managers have the communication skills to have appropriate conversations with individuals about their precise fears. Where there are particular cultural features which you discover are important to people, it may be worth communicating if they are to be allowed to continue. For example, there may be a custom that people always have a birthday cake and a small party in their department when it is their birthday, or that people are allowed to bring their dogs into work. Reassuring people that these practices can continue shows both that you are listening to their concerns and that you care about them.

Table 5.2   *Concluded*

Part of the pain of change for people is the loss of control. Over time they will have established a degree of control over their daily lives which change threatens.	It is important to be clear where people can continue to control their working environments. Give people as much opportunity to control it as possible, or at least make sure they can contribute to discussions about it. The more people are able to take the initiative in driving change for themselves, the lower the resistance due to loss of control will be.
Lack of confidence in the prospects of success	
Longer-serving people and managers in particular have progressed in the organisation with the skills and knowledge that they have. If new skills and knowledge are going to be necessary in the future they may well lack confidence that they are going to master these new ones and thrive.	Again, the actual delivery of support for people to master new skills lies outside your remit. What you can do is make sure that people know what support is available for personal development and how seriously the new organisation takes its responsibilities for equipping people with new skills.
There may also be fears over "soft" issues such as people losing standing both in their own eyes and in those of their colleagues or family and friends outside work.	Your role as a communicator is to make sure that managers at every level understand the importance of maintaining people's self-image in order to reduce resistance to change. There may also be practical issues to help people sustain their status externally, such as allowing people to keep job titles or other perks which cost little or nothing but mean a great deal to the individuals concerned. You also have a role in giving people some alternative pride in the new organisation. Much of this will be done at a later stage (see Stage 6), but the tone and messages of the first 100 days should at least be giving people a pride that they belong to a great new organisation.

Understanding the real drivers

In one airline, a merger resulted in an excess of captains. It was agreed that they would fly as first officers, retaining their pay and allowances as captains. They were, however, worried that their neighbours would see them leaving for work wearing a first officer's uniform and think worse of them. It was agreed that they could keep their captain's uniforms.

General implications of potential resistance for communicating and managing change

1.   Communication about the need for change needs to be compelling and credible. It needs to provide people with the information they need to draw their own conclusions, and provide them with the space to do this rather than haranguing people with views from senior management.

2.   You need to have adult-to-adult conversations, many of them one-on-one and really to listen to the individual concerns people have.

3.   People need to understand that change is inevitable. As long as they think that really they can go back to how things were, they will hanker after the old ways.

Among the tasks of communication are to explain:

•   Why the organisation needs to change because of the environment in which it is operating. The more external sources that you expose people to the better. In our era of low trust people will often only believe something when the sources are numerous as well as independently credible. The earlier people have information about the external environment the better. Ideally the more intelligent and well-informed people in the organisation should be saying to each other and to the management that they think the company should this about changing, even before the company has put its own point of view.

•   Why the alternatives are not viable or, if they are viable, why they have not been preferred. It is not enough to make a case for change in this cynical age – one must also make the case against alternatives, including the option of sticking with the old ways.

The whole issue of changing attitudes in a broader sense is covered in the Chapter 6.

Communication Overload

One of the problems is likely to be the sheer volume of material to communicate. Without careful control people will be deluged and paradoxically feel ill informed under a welter of information. Not only is there likely to be a mass of announcements and changes of practice or procedure to communicate arising out of the merger or acquisition itself, but with the pace of change in most organisations the chances are there are other major change programmes continuing at the same time.

In addition, as we have seen, it is important for you to show that you understand how employees are feeling and what their concerns are at this time. The danger is that the big message – about the rationale for the deal – can be lost.

Targeting

One of the secrets of managing volume of communication is targeting information. Later in this chapter we look at the very different sorts of audience in the first 100 days, and although audiences inevitably overlap and talk to each other, targeting information so that it reaches only those who want it can help.

Obviously, in many ways the ideal person to decide what any individual needs to know is the person themself. Increasingly, software products are being developed which allow people to register their interest for particular categories of information, so that they can in effect target themselves. As this becomes available it will make the communicator's life easier, as all you will need to do is make sure each item is properly labelled, and people will access it for themselves on demand. "Pull" targeting by individuals is a key ingredient of avoiding overload, especially if there are good means of indicating who an item will be of most value to and its relative importance.

There are, however, some difficulties with this approach:

- It may make it harder to shape messages specifically for each audience if the categories are fairly general. People may have very different sorts of interest in types of information and have to spend some time sorting through to find the parts that are useful to them.

- It relies on people having the time and motivation actually to read the material that finds itself on their front page or in their inbox (depending on the technology). If they have wide interests they may be deluged even with information they have themselves sought.

- It makes it hard to push information which you may want them to read or understand but for which they currently have no thirst. This is particularly likely to be the big picture information, which, as we have seen, is vital to people's understanding of the need for change. In a busy day, with immediate pressures to perform, people are unlikely to find time to read information of marginal immediate interest.

The simplest way to target information is to give managers the task of filtering the mass of communication and passing on to their teams what is most relevant to them. This has the merit that managers are more likely than anyone, except the people themselves, to know what they need to know. The problems are:

- Managers rarely have the time themselves to read through the available information so they often either don't read it at all or take so long to do so that the information is old by the time they pass it on.

- Managers often lack the skills or imagination to think through properly what will be relevant and how best to communicate it to the various members of their teams.

- There is a danger that different managers make different decisions about what to pass on, with the result that people can find themselves not knowing something that colleagues in other departments know, and the grapevine finds fertile territory as colleagues confer and attempt to fill in the gaps.

One of the essential features is to distinguish, for each of your distinct audiences, which are the absolutely vital issues they need to understand from the rest of the material which may be of lesser interest or use.

Another element of minimising overload is to minimise the messages coming from the top. New chief executives are often keen to publicise their values and vision for the new organisation. Our advice is to hold on this until the first rush of communication is over and people have more time. Now is the time to keep reiterating the reasons for the deal. The senior management will be utterly bored with the message by now and want to move on to the next thing. But your audiences will not have heard it so often and, as they deal with the discomfort of change, will need constant reminders about why it is necessary or worthwhile. There is likely to be more than enough detail and novelty to communicate without touching on new big picture material.

Projects and workstreams

Most of the detailed work at this stage is done in projects and workstreams, some of which may have started before Day One. These projects are both an opportunity and a challenge for the communicator.

There is, of course, an enormous variety in the sorts and scale of workstreams or projects that organisations use in the first 100 days. The presumption in the following observations is that employees from both parts of the organisation will be involved at some stage and that there is some sort of hierarchy of projects whereby detailed work is devolved to groups of people who really know the intricacies of the new ways of working they are helping to design. Depending on the scale of the integration, some of the workstreams may last far longer than the magic 100-day figure, but the communication issues are similar regardless of when the workstreams are generating their decisions.

On the one hand, as we have seen, the more people can be involved in change, and be part of designing it, the easier it is for them to accept it. There is also an advantage in building relationships across the new organisation as people work together to solve problems. There are, however, potential dangers which the communicator needs to be aware of and avert:

- them-and-us attitudes within the workstreams;

- no involvement of people not actually in the workstream, causing an information vacuum;

- the opposite problem of rumours flying from the workstreams;

- overlapping workstreams or inconsistent decisions being made by them;

- feelings of betrayal if recommendations by the projects or workstreams are not accepted.

The are several things that you can do to avert these:

- Ensure that workstreams or project teams have absolutely clear terms of reference, and know what the boundaries of their remits are. This is particularly important where front-line staff have been given the opportunity to help solve operational or morale problems. Any potential good the teams can have, in informing, involving and building relationships, can be lost if the team finds that its recommendations are unacceptable because they are not in accordance with some wider plan or limits which were not clear in the first place. If there are "right answers" which you are waiting for the teams to come up with on their own, they will soon realise that they are being manipulated. Where the organisation is clear exactly what it wants, it should say so and give the workstream the tasks of working on implementation or deciding the detail.

- Encourage the people in the workstreams to seek information from relevant sources in both previous organisations. It is then important to manage the communication in and out of the inner teams. It can be helpful to communicate to the whole organisation at the outset that teams will be asking questions and investigating possibilities, many of which will probably never come to pass. People should be asked not to speculate or discuss with colleagues the questions they have been asked or the information that has been sought.

- Make sure that the workstreams have an established communication methodology, which a member of your team, or at least a trained communicator, controls. The outputs from the various workstreams need to be coordinated and managed for the various audiences (see section on managing volume). It should be made clear to project group members what information is confidential, what is available should people ask and what is being actively communicated.

- To prevent the "them and us" or "our way is better" syndromes, it is necessary to do some explicit work with the team members about understanding what is happening to culture in the new organisation.

- The whole business of communicating from workstreams is easier if there is an integration manager liaising between the groups and dealing with potential overlaps or contradictions. If there is not, you may be doing some of their work by deciding on the most important messages and clarifying any apparent contradictions. It is also your role to alert more senior management if there are conflicts or contradictions, which may be apparent to you before anyone else as you are being asked to coordinate the messages.

- Whether or not there is an integration manager you will need to keep an overall view of the timetable of outputs from the various groups, so that communication can be planned across the different media to the various audiences.

- While there is a mass of work being done, it will be useful to have gatekeepers for certain audiences. One simple discipline is to track the information that specific groups of employees may be getting. This can be done using databases or even spreadsheets; a tool like this can ensure that people are not being expected to take in more than is reasonable and that messages have some consistency.

- Some managers are likely to be so busy at this time that they will have difficulty thinking ahead and may be thinking about themselves and their personal futures to the detriment of their teams. It is the communicator's job to make sure the messages are easy for them to communicate. For senior people you may need to do some work helping them see the wood for the trees.

Collating and channelling information for particular audiences

When RBS bought NatWest Bank in 2001, many processes and IT systems were brought together as part of the integration process. This meant many working changes for customers and staff. For the 1,500 customer relationship managers (RMs) in Business Banking, this meant detailed changes on a weekly basis that they needed information for, and copies of relevant customer communication.

The myriad changes and associated internal and customer communication could have drowned the busy RMs, especially as they were also receiving business as usual communication.

All relevant changes agreed were collected as communication packs specially designed for the RMs, pulling together all the information needed, including copies of the letters which would be sent to customers. Where relevant these were personalised for the RM with a list of their customers affected by each change and the associated customer communication, plus any staff actions needed.

Other, less essential information, was available through the intranet, but the information they needed to know for their essential customer relationships was collated and targeted specifically for them.

Other overload issues

Beware of inward focus at this time. There will be so much internal material to communicate, with the outputs of workstreams, appointments and practical changes to working methods, that there is a danger the organisation forgets its need to look after its external stakeholders. You need to make sure that you leave room in the mass of communication for enough content about delivering the experience customers expect, and do not allow yourselves to become distracted from meeting operational targets. This is sometimes referred to as the challenge of changing the wheels while the car is in motion.

A further challenge relating to overload is the fact that former leaders are likely to continue to communicate to their former teams, if they are still around to communicate. This can be one of the dangers of keeping senior or middle managers from the target who may feel hurt or angry by the deal. They may continue to pour out negative messages to their former staff, whether or not those staff are still working for them. It is difficult to stop this activity, but there are various alternative strategies you can use:

- If these people are really poisoning new relationships you may rethink the wisdom of keeping them in the new organisation and consider that money spent on freeing the organisation from their pernicious influence may be money well spent.

- Make sure that there are alternative and convincing arguments being put forward, backed by incontrovertible facts, so that the credibility of the negative messages is minimised.

- Make sure that influential senior people of a more positive frame of mind establish face-to-face communication with people in the former target, if possible with a social element so that new relationships are built.

- Make sure that you are not genuinely at fault, thus giving your detractors ammunition to attack you with. Listen carefully to their allegations and if possible draw the detractors in to helping solve the problems.

- If the problems come from unresolved board or executive team disagreements, do not allow these disagreements to be swept under the table. Get some external help if necessary to help them agree a way forward to which the top team are all genuinely committed. Disagreements at that level will continue to cause confusion if they are allowed to continue.

It is worth making sure that the channels you are using for communication encourage people to think through the changes for themselves, rather than merely having them and the reasons explained to them. This requires a discussion-based approach, asking people to understand the context and alternative ways forward.

Appointments and Structural Changes

There can be difficulties with communication and relationships over appointments for new jobs, however you play it. If you rush into making appointments you have the advantage of getting the misery over with quickly but are unlikely to be able to prove that you have been fair; if you have a long-drawn-out process you have the opposite advantages and disadvantages. In addition, through a long-drawn-out-process competitors for management jobs will have to work with each other on integration matters, which can prove tense and have negative impacts on their ability to communicate with their teams. Whichever you go for, you need to explain the rationale while being open about the shortcomings of the method.

As appointments are made and structures are changed people may feel they are in limbo. Make sure they always know who their boss is – even if only for this week – and what the team is trying to achieve.

There are, of course, logistical challenges in communicating appointments. It is important to get to disappointed applicants in advance of the rest, and to others immediately affected quickly. A mistake which we often see made is to communicate appointments to everyone. This can be a major element of overload. It is important to distinguish the few people who need to have the information actively "pushed" at them from those who merely need to be able to "pull" information if they need to look it up.

The people to whom appointments should be actively communicated are:

- people currently working for the manager being given another appointment;

- people who will work for the new appointee.

The information needs to include a little about the appointee and their career to date. It is also helpful if you can give details about when they are to start in the new job and when people will hear about the filling of the post behind them.

For the "pull" information suitable channels are:

- intranet round-up of recent appointments;

- magazine or newsletter round-up or summary.

It is also essential to keep organisation charts up to date on the intranet, including future job holders' names as soon as they are known. If you are undertaking major reorganisation you may need two complete sets of organisation charts – one for the "old" organisation and the other for the new, showing job holders as they are announced.

If you are running a team briefing system which requires managers to do a key job in communicating with their teams, it will be important to keep lists up to date so that you know who is briefing whom. There can be a huge impact on teams losing a trusted long-term leader who moves to another job within the new organisation. Their former staff may feel deserted and lost; it is essential that you ensure the new leader, however temporary, takes on responsibility for communicating with this team and taking on board their concerns. If there is an interregnum make sure that the manager's manager or a colleague knows that they have the responsibility of briefing the team.

There may also be a challenge communicating the departure of people you would rather had not left, in particular stars previously feted in the organisation. This might include top sales people or the specialist professionals who make the value in your organisation, such as research scientists or fund managers. These people often have great influence, and their leaving can start a trend. When making the announcements you need to make it clear that there is plenty of other talent around and remind people of the exciting work to be done. Even if you have not identified key people in the due diligence phase or in the gap between announcement and completion, it may be worth doing so now so that you can plan individual communication with them and not lose them unnecessarily.

Communicating Redundancy

The new organisation will have to make a number of decisions about redundancy if, as is usually the case, there are some savings to be make from integration. These are mainly HR decisions, including:

- Are there only named posts to go (for example, in management and finance)? If so, will the individuals simply be made redundant, or will you offer redundancy more generally and allow people in posts at risk to apply for other posts thereby vacated?

- Are you going to offer voluntary redundancy? If so, are there some people who will not be offered it? What are you going to do if you get too many volunteers? You need to be careful not to give the impression that everyone will be allowed to go if they will not. It can be extremely demotivating for people to psych themselves up for a new career with their redundancy pay only to be told that redundancy terms are not available for them.

- Are you guaranteeing no compulsory redundancy? If so, what are you going to do if you get too few volunteers?

- If there is compulsory redundancy, what are the selection criteria?

In addition to the requirements of the Transfer of Undertakings regulations, there is a requirement to consult employees in the event of making more than 20 people redundant. Employers are obliged to communicate to representatives, in writing, the reasons for the proposals, numbers affected, selection criteria and timing.

There is always a dilemma about how much to tell representatives in confidence and how much to share with everyone. Our advice would be to communicate actively as much as possible to everyone; people are bound to be interested and will guess answers to these questions if you do not tell them. The only exception is information relating to individuals, where obviously it is essential that representatives hold anything you tell them in confidence, at least until the individuals have been consulted. It is important to set the confidentiality rules with the representatives at the outset. They will be keen to have everything clear about what they can pass on and what they cannot, as their constituents will be pressing them for information.

It can be useful – indeed essential – to be able to share information that, in practice, relates to individuals, for example, if there are only one or two people with a particular job title and you are talking about the possibility of that role ceasing to exist. It is helpful to be able to discuss alternatives with the representatives before consulting with the individuals, who might be spared unnecessary worry. If you are to have genuine open-minded consultation with representatives it is important that you all recognise the importance of keeping confidences until you are ready to communicate in a planned and considerate way.

You will, of course, need to have a plan for dealing with leaks or, more likely, guesses. At a time like this people are bound to exchange guesses about what they would do; these guesses quickly become rumours and you cannot ignore them. It is important, however, not to be bounced into inappropriate communication in response to a question or a rumour. You should acknowledge that there are rumours and guesswork and assure people that once you have a clear plan there will be communication and consultation with individuals. Tell people that anything they hear in advance of the formal communication is not reliable.

Of course, the better the communication in general, the easier the communication of redundancy is. Where people are well informed about the issues facing the business and its competitive context they may well expect job losses following the deal, and gradually will have acclimatised themselves to the notion that they may have to seek work elsewhere. They are likely to have started to think about the opportunities as well as the trauma. The announcement about actual redundancies will come as no surprise and there will therefore probably be less anger and shock than if the announcements come out of a communication vacuum.

For those facing redundancy

The timing of the announcements about particular posts or categories of employee at risk is extremely delicate. When people are hurt they naturally look for someone to blame, and any slight flaw in the way they were told will be relayed and amplified around the organisation. Naturally people prefer to have such an emotive message told them face-to-face and individually by someone who knows them and can handle the meeting sensitively. The logistics of this are not always easy to handle:

- If there are just a few people going, in specific roles, then ideally they should be seen individually, typically by their immediate manager with some HR support. The rest of the team should be told immediately afterwards, with the individual being given the bad news having the option of attending or not.

- If more than one person is going, and particularly if it is not clear which individuals are going but simply a number and a category, then the group should be seen together. They should be told the rationale for the decision and the criteria for selection, and assured that they will have a one-to-one discussion within the next day or so.

- If there is a whole site or whole department to go, then inevitably there will have to be an announcement to the whole group.

Whether people are told as individuals or as a group, they are likely still to be so shocked – even if they thought they were expecting it – that they will not be capable of taking in much other information. It is important therefore that you give them access to the information they will seek once the immediate shock is passed, such as:

- How much they will get in redundancy pay?

- What will happen to their pension?

- What help they will get in finding another job?

- How to organise time off to look for another job?

- Who they can talk to in confidence about personal difficulties this presents? (for example, through an Employee Assistance Plan or other provision of welfare or counselling help).

- When will they actually leave the business? (or how the date will be decided), including if there are financial penalties for leaving earlier than the date stated.

You will need to make sure there are a number of channels for this information. At least one should be written, so that people can take it home as well as looking at it while at work. It is useful to have a helpline available too, by telephone as well as online. When people are emotional it can sometimes be hard for them to express themselves succinctly in writing, so a live human being, who can ask questions for clarification, can often give fuller answers than a web-based helpline.

Most importantly, you will need to make sure that immediate managers are equipped for the whole communication exercise, including both the original breaking of the news and the follow-up individual interviews. Whether people have been told individually or in a group, they will need time alone with their immediate manager to talk through the implications, for managers to reiterate the reasons and for the individuals to express their feelings and ask their questions.

Checklist: Equipping managers to communicate the decision

- Provide plenty of advance coaching support in giving bad news and helping people to manage change.

- In spite of the fact that people will find it hard to take in at this stage, the reasons for the redundancies need to be reiterated. At the same time it is important that people feel that their previous contributions to the organisation have been recognised and appreciated.

- Educate managers in people's likely reaction to bad news – fear, anger and so on: so they are aware these feelings are likely to be directed at them, but that this is natural. Support them in thinking through coping mechanisms.

- Where managers communicating the decision are not the decision-takers, provide an opportunity for them to understand the detail of the rationale and decisions in depth, with sessions encouraging managers to raise all the questions they have and that their people are likely to ask, and allowing them to express their views and concerns.

- Where managers are also the decision-takers, provide coaching and practice in not reacting defensively when contrary views are expressed.

- Reinforce the importance of managers supporting the decisions when talking with their team. Provide opportunities for challenge in private, and equip managers with deep understanding of the rationale so that they can focus on that in subsequent discussions.

- Provide a detailed timetable for the announcement plus a "bullet point" script of key points for managers to follow.

- Provide managers with a "help point" (for example a phone line to HR) for immediate questions and support during the announcement process.

- Acknowledge that the process is traumatic for the managers who have to give the news, as well as for the individuals who receive it. They themselves may need support through a mentor or buddy system or from their own line managers giving them time to talk through the experience.

- Provide information about the specific questions people are likely to ask.

- Build understanding of the need to reinforce messages.

- Help managers to think through and recognise the different needs of stayers and leavers and how each can best be met.

When people do not like the message they are being given there is a natural tendency to blame the communication rather than the message. Inevitably then, if the redundancies are unpopular, there will be people saying they were badly communicated with, however well you do it. Inevitably, too, if there are many job loss conversations in the organisation, some of them will be handled badly in spite of your best efforts. All you can do is make sure that you have done all you can to support managers with material and training and not to get too demoralised when you hear the occasional inevitable complaint.

In terms of the number of jobs to go, be aware that turnover is likely to increase naturally in the months following a merger or acquisition. Many organisations find themselves in the expensive and embarrassing position of making people redundant and then having to go back and re-hire a few months later. This is obviously a matter for your HR colleagues, but since it damages credibility as well as profitability to have to recruit soon after a redundancy exercise, you have a responsibility to ask questions. Apart from anything else, people are bound to ask what turnover you are presuming when calculating numbers.

In many cases it will not be clear immediately how many jobs will need to go. Decisions may wait on projects or workstreams which will run longer than the first 100 days, and often the merger or acquisition itself takes place in a turbulent market, where decisions are affected not only by potential integration savings but also by falling sales. In the communication of a first tranche of redundancies therefore you need to be careful not to give the impression that there will be no further cuts. This is a hard one to manage. One of the first questions that survivors will ask is: "Are there more cuts to come?" If you say no, it is sure to be proved untrue later, at a serious cost to your credibility. If you say yes, people will just be waiting for the next announcement. All you can do is be as open as possible about the process so that people can think through the implications for themselves.

For the rest of the organisation

The organisation of communication to those affected by redundancy is often so demanding, both emotionally and logistically, that the communication needs of the stayers or survivors are ignored. This is a serious mistake. The view that survivors have of the organisation will be strongly influenced by how they believe the leavers have been treated. They will want to know that people were treated fairly and with dignity. Unhappy people inevitably will tell many colleagues about their perceived mistreatment, and you cannot defend yourself case by case. Again all you can do is make sure that people have been fairly treated. It is also worth discussing with your HR and line colleagues, if there are very angry or unhappy people working out their notice or consultation periods, whether the organisation would be better to pay them off rather than allowing them to come in and demoralise their colleagues.

It is also important that there is ongoing communication for the people who are staying. They need to feel that they have made the right choice in staying with the organisation and that both it and they have great futures. Do not let the communication channels be overwhelmed with information for leavers to the detriment of these messages for those who are staying.

When people are leaving the business in quite high numbers it is sometimes difficult to know how to communicate who is going. There is a temptation to just let people slip away so as to avoid focusing attention on how many are going, but this is a mistake. Having people disappear without announcement at dead of night will seem like the Stasi; it makes for insecurity and it demonstrates a lack of value for the people going. It is important to note the passing of people, with regular lists of leavers in whatever channel you usually use for this information, thanking them for their contributions over the years.

For customers and other external stakeholders

Where the people going have pivotal relationships with customers or suppliers it is important that the relationship is not damaged. It is essential that the victim is not their only source of information about the changes. Preferably before the victim themself does so, a more senior person from the company needs to make personal contact (by telephone or face-to-face) with the key individuals. They will need a script or an outline of what to say, which should include the organisation's continuing valuing of the relationship and the name of their new contact. If possible the new person should be introduced at once, with the senior person also being available to the customer or supplier.

If the customer or supplier usually deals with a number of different people, for instance through a customer centre, the agents may also need to be given a script or some key points to make in response to queries. If not, they are placed in an awkward situation when an outside contact asks something like, "What happened to so-and-so who used to —? I've heard since the merger you've been getting rid of a lot of people. I suppose this means you won't be interested in —." Your internal communication needs to be giving people throughout the organisation confidence to deal with this inevitable conversation.

Communicating Business as Usual

Whatever the degree of communication emerging out of the merger or acquisition, it is important not to lose the plot on ongoing communication. In a study of 193 mergers during the 1990s the Cox School of Business found that only 37 per cent of acquired companies maintained revenue growth in the first quarter after the merger. You need to keep communication going at both corporate and local levels.

At a corporate level people need to be reminded of the ongoing need to keep the business going, keep the customers happy, keep gaining new customers, keep quality up, keep costs down, and so on. If you are not careful these ongoing messages may be forgotten. As in ordinary times, people need to know what difference their contribution makes. Bill Quirke (1995) quotes research showing that 91 per cent of employees who understand what makes their business successful want to work towards its success, compared with only 23 per cent of those who do not understand their role.

Ongoing communication is at least as important at a local level. Where there is change everywhere, people need to be focused on the work they do rather than on the rumours or even the news of major upheaval. Having measures of team performance is essential, so that teams can get a sense of achievement or urgency at a level that they demonstrably contribute to.

Given the rapid pace of change in organisations in the twenty-first century there are likely to be other changes, perhaps major ones, happening at the same time as the merger integration. If the buyer is a serial acquirer there may still be digestion work going on from the previous merger, with the tail end of integration projects still churning out changes. If the merger was driven by a change in technology, competitive activity or a change in the markets there may well be projects already working to react to these changes and or cut costs.

The basic disciplines of things like up-to-date organisation charts and phone lists on the intranet may require a particular effort at this time, and are especially important. They may change frequently but even if they only hold true for a few days it is good for your credibility, as well as useful to the organisation, to make the investment in getting them right.

There is a danger that creativity and innovation can be lost at this time, as they are adversely affected by disruption and stress. If possible you should generate excitement about the new organisation and encourage managers to use the novelty of new teams to prevent this happening.

Coordinating messages in a time of change

In Pfizer, at the time of its acquisition of Pharmacia in 2003, there was a major project to improve productivity and reallocate resources from support functions such as IT and HR to science and projects.

The communication team coordinated the announcements from both projects so that there were not two sets of communication confusing people. It was frustrating that the acquisition delayed some of the decisions on the productivity project, but they were able to announce a clear timetable of decision-making.

THE DIFFERENT INTERNAL AUDIENCES

In addition to the explicit messages which you will be sending to employees in the first 100 days, employees will be actively looking for implicit messages.

The tone as well as the content of every statement needs to be carefully crafted at this stage. It is also useful to think about the different states of mind of different parts of the audience. Any one person, of course, falls into more than one category of audience, so you need to avoid inconsistencies even as you are aware of the different psychological states and preoccupations of different groups.

Likely classifications include:

- legacy bidder organisation;
- legacy target organisation;
- people in parts of organisation scheduled for quick integration;
- people in parts of organisation not scheduled for any immediate change;
- high-flyers who you are particularly keen to keep;
- people who already know they will leave the new organisation;
- opinion leaders;
- employee representatives;
- managers, especially middle managers, who must keep the current business going;
- customer-facing staff;
- alumni.

Legacy Bidder Organisation

People in the legacy bidder organisation may be feeling arrogant and triumphant, and may not expect to be affected at all by forthcoming changes. These first three months or so are also a vital time to communicate with them if they are likely to be affected in the longer run. There is a short window for them when their ears are temporarily open to messages about the nature of the new organisation; after this time they will assume that everything is going to be as before, in the absence of clear communication. They may well feel betrayed later if changes are made which start to affect them, too.

There is a strange psychology at work which can make people in the bidder organisation feel superior to those in the target and lord it over them almost as if they were an occupying army. It is your job to stem this arrogance. It is sometimes made even harder by the fact that the acquiring organisation may have invested more than the target, not just in physical assets but in its people too. People in the bidder organisation may genuinely be better trained to do their jobs, more knowledgeable and more confident. This does not mean, of course, that the people in the target organisation cannot become equally competent given the right investment.

This can be a difficult message to convey, especially as people in the target organisation will be feeling sensitive and alert for any signs of condescension or arrogance. In the long run, of course, it is good news for the people in the target organisation as they will have access to the same superior opportunities that their counterparts have, but in the short run their disadvantage may make their jobs less secure and leave their self-esteem battered. It is worth pointing out that there will be individuals in both organisations who do not fit this stereotype and that people should not prejudge any individual with whom they will have dealings. Managers at every level set an example over relationships with new colleagues; they need to understand the importance of their attitude and language.

Legacy Target Organisation

Even if there is no sense of superiority from the acquirers, emotions in the target will be raw at this time. The organisation they chose to join, and with which they identified to a greater or lesser degree, has ceased to exist. They will fear and expect to be devalued, for their ways of doing things to be denigrated and possibly for their jobs to be lost. They are unlikely to be hearing any messages with cold rationality. When people are upset they cease to listen or to process new information. The implications for the communicator of this excess of emotion is that messages need to be repeated often so that recipients can hear them when they are ready. You also need to have plenty of channels to listen to people's hurt and to show empathy, as it may be they will only be able to listen to what the organisation has to say when they feel they themselves have been heard.

There is also a real danger that there is a sort of vicious circle of loss of confidence among people in the target organisation, whereby a view that they are not valued can eventually lead to a self-fulfilling prophesy.

It is particularly important, once again, to equip managers with the ability to hold individual conversations with people, and to make sure that HR specialists around the business have the time and knowledge to talk to people individually about their personal hopes and fears.

Where Quick Integration is Scheduled

As we know, people tend to listen to all news following a merger or acquisition with two ears: one for the organisation and one for themselves. For those in the first wave of integration, the ear listening out for personal implications will be dominant. Your problem as a communicator is that you probably don't have the answers to the questions people are asking: *Will I have a job? If so where, what will the prospects be? Who will my boss be? What will the work be like?* There are only two things you can do:

1. Explain the decision-making process and timetable if possible. If there is a relevant workstream tell people who the members of it are, what its objectives are, who will sign off decisions and most importantly, what is the timescale for decision-making. If there is a selection process going on, people will again want to know what the process is, who makes the decisions and on what grounds, and when will they know the outcome. There is also, of course, the practical detail which people need to know if they have to apply for jobs in the new integrated team, such as what sort of application they need to make to whom by when.

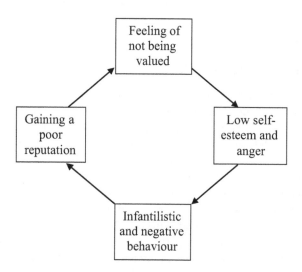

Figure 5.2   **Loss of confidence among people in the target organisation**

2.   As decisions are made, make sure that you have speedy ways of disseminating them, which work at the same pace for all the affected parties. We saw that one of the things to do in the run up to Day One was to make sure that these channels existed for all employees. Email works brilliantly for some populations and the temptation is to think it works for everyone. Where it doesn't reach (for example for people who do not work at PCs), old-fashioned noticeboards can work well if they are properly managed. For people who do not come into an office or depot regularly and do not use email you may need to arrange for them to be telephoned individually, for very important announcements, or write to them at home.

Of course, once the immediate announcements have been made you need to be ready both to explain details and rationale more fully in a written form to which people can refer and to have the channels available for people to ask questions or express views (see later section for further discussion of your toolkit at this stage).

People in Parts of the Organisation not Immediately Affected

There are two opposite dangers here. The first is that people are living in unnecessary immediate fear, which may lead to their wasting time worrying and sharing concerns with colleagues, looking for alternative employment or just not concentrating on the work they should be doing. The other is that they feel they are completely safe, that they have somehow escaped the consequences of the merger or acquisition and that life will carry on as before. The only problem with this second danger is that it makes it harder for them to accept change when their turn comes around.

Inevitably your attention will be focused elsewhere during the first 100 days, but in communication to the whole organisation it is worth bearing in mind the need to avoid these opposite dangers.

High-Flyers You are Keen to Keep

Headhunters will be circling your organisation like vultures around a kill. The people you most need to keep for the long-term success of the organisation will be the ones they are most likely to pick off. You need individual and targeted communication with each one of them. This, of course, is something that you need to work on with your HR colleagues, who will have identified the relevant people. Much of the communication with them needs to be on a one-to-one basis by people who are influential in the new organisation and will be seen by the high-flyers as useful potential allies for the future. However, it can also help to direct more general communication about the vision for the organisation.

In some cases informal occasions can be arranged for high-flyers to meet with senior people, for example by travelling together to another site, or for meals. Personal contact time is often a key element to keeping these people, and will ensure that you understand their individual needs well enough to provide them with the right blend of challenge and reward.

People Who Already Know They Will Leave the Organisation

In many organisations people leave as soon as the decision has been made for them to go, but in many M&A situations this may not be practical, as work must go on until new arrangements have been put in place. You may have announced, for example, the closing of an office with a date six months in the future. It is important that the staff there continue to work well and enthusiastically for the short period that they are still with you. This is not impossible.

High productivity on a site in the period of run-down

In one organisation we worked with, the Group announced the closure of the site with two years' notice. There was a strong communication campaign which concentrated on walking out with "heads held high", having their best ever quality and productivity levels. At the same time they made sure that everyone received first-rate opportunities both to train for subsequent jobs and to obtain advice about getting later work.

The site succeeded in maintaining its targets right up to the closure date.

Not only do leavers continue to provide a service or make product where quality needs to be maintained, but their attitudes inevitably spill over to their colleagues who are staying. If leavers are constantly expressing anger and holding forth on how badly they think they or their colleagues have been treated, it will have an influence on the views of a much wider range of people than those immediately affected.

Treating leavers well – and having them say so – also gives people confidence that, should the business ever need to close their site or otherwise dispose of their services, they would be well treated and need not fear ongoing unemployment.

Opinion Leaders

Some organisations have gone to the extent of trying to identify opinion leaders so that, rather than dissipate communication effort on everyone, they concentrate it on the people others are most likely to listen to.

This can be a useful additional means of communication, but be careful not to use opinion leaders as a channel in competition to the management line.

Managers are accountable to the organisation for how they communicate; opinion leaders may feel they have more to lose by pushing an unpopular message and may put a spin on it which preserves their popularity rather than ensuring the credibility of the message itself.

It can also be extremely detrimental to managers to use others to communicate. In the first place, it can disempower managers if they know less of what is going on than the "ambassadors" or "champions"; secondly, the person who does the communicating is inevitably seen as a leader by the team, as they are the people with the answers to questions. This leaves the manager without the leadership role in the team.

One way of gaining the advantages of drawing opinion leaders into the communication process without reducing the communication role of managers is to use them as a sounding board. They can tell you what the likely reaction of other employees is likely to be, help you present information in the way most likely to be heeded and, by being implicated in the creation of material, are likely to support it when questioned by colleagues after material is disseminated. There are innumerable ways of doing this, from formal elected bodies to informal focus groups.

Employee Representatives

In many ways these are similar to the opinion leaders described in the last section. They are likely to be opinion leaders, otherwise they would not have been elected by their members. There are, of course, legal requirements for consultation with elected employee representatives.

Middle Managers

Middle managers are a key group for two reasons: first, they are inevitably opinion leaders themselves, usually with formal as well as informal communication roles; second, they are the people who are most responsible for maintaining the performance of the organisation. If they feel disaffected or ill informed the knock-on consequences can be disastrous.

The challenge is that, as well as being a key group, they are often among the most adversely affected by the merger. While top management are the most likely to lose their jobs, they are also likely to be the biggest winners in terms of pay-offs. Middle managers are more at risk than other groups, as jobs are often duplicated across the two organisations, while they are rarely in the fat cat league of pay-offs. Also, unlike the most senior managers, their fate is often not clear immediately and they have to live with uncertainty for some time. In many cases, too, they will explicitly be competing for jobs. In other cases they will already know that they do not have a future in the new organisation but are continuing to do their jobs until their release date.

Whether or not they are staying with the organisation, the important message for middle managers is that they and the contribution they have made to the organisation, and that they continue to make in their day-to-day work, are valued. They also need to be crystal clear themselves about the rationale for change and confident that they are well informed or have easy access to all the information they need. Keeping middle managers feeling that they are valued and well informed will take time, with senior managers communicating face-to-face. Your job is to make sure that:

- senior managers are given guidance so that they run enough and appropriate one-to-one meetings, conferences and management team meetings;

- senior managers are equipped with material and support to run meetings that have the desired effect.

In addition, you need to be aware of the likely attitudes of individual middle managers if they are part of your communication framework. If they themselves are disaffected they should not be used to communicate sensitive messages, especially those which may be perceived to affect them negatively.

Don't let the victims do the communicating

In one organisation, reorganisation following a merger centralised an area of work which was formerly done in the regions. Even though there were no job losses in the regions, the regional managers perceived that they were losing power and prestige.

They were left to present the change to their teams, which they did putting a negative spin on the changes, leaving most staff in the regions convinced that it was a bad decision.

Especially where managers perceive that they are competing for jobs, the atmosphere in the first 100 days is likely to be extremely political. You need to be providing a very clear line about decisions that are made, otherwise managers may well use the announcements in effect to brief against each other.

Hubbard (2001) points out the different concerns that different categories of people have during mergers. Front-line employees are primarily worried about job security, the well-being of their work group and colleagues, changes to their own role and status and changes in the corporate culture. Top managers, on the other hand, are less concerned about their colleagues. The concerns of managers change in the months following the acquisition. While both middle and senior managers are primarily interested in individual matters at the time of the announcement, middle managers turn their attention to group matters during implementation. Hubbard points out what a key group middle managers are and how important it is to the success of the implementation that they are happy about how they perceive their colleagues are being treated.

We have seen that personal chemistry is immensely important at the deal-making stage between the chief protagonists. It is accepted that the human factor is a real issue at this stage. The same allowance for human frailty is more rarely seen during the first 100 days and subsequent integration, when people are expected just to be professional and get on with the job in hand without being distracted by emotions.

Customer-facing Staff

Customer-facing staff will need to be confident that they can answer questions from their customers or clients. It is important therefore that they have the stories they need in response to any articles in the public and, particularly, trade media. It will be important to offer face-to-face communication or even role plays so that people have a chance to resolve any queries they may have themselves as well as those they think their customers may confront them with.

Alumni

One of the challenges you face as communicator is that alumni are likely to continue to have an influence over employees. This is particularly the case if they are senior level people and if they have left recently. You may think that you have rid the organisation of the baneful influence of some of the people who remain angry or upset by the deal once they have left the organisation, but often they continue to have informal channels to reach your people.

There are only three things you can do about this:

1.   Continue to communicate with them even after they have left. Most organisations do not keep a database of previous employees and the only way to reach them is through the pension scheme if they are members of it. The big consultancies are good at keeping in touch with alumni, sending them publications and inviting them to events where they are given presentations about ongoing developments. Of course, they are also potential clients for the consultancies, but this is a model which is useful to follow in the aftermath of a merger.

2.   Make the internal communication as compelling, emotional and personal as the negative alumni messages.

3.   On occasion it can be necessary to brief managers not to leak information to previous employees and not to depress themselves by listening to them.

YOUR TOOLKIT AT THIS STAGE

Table 5.3   Channels of communication for different categories of employees

	Urgent	Background
Office-based staff.	Email.	Team meetings, publications, bigger meetings as appropriate.
Shop floor or other employees without PC on desk.	Noticeboards.	
Home-based staff.	Email.	
On the road (for example, sales or service repair).	Telephone or (if less urgent or emotive) letters to home address.	
Shift workers.	Depends on shifts. If announcement affects them and they are not coming on site within 24 hours then need to telephone individually.	
People on maternity leave or long-term sick leave.	Telephone or (if less urgent or emotive) letters to home address.	

Email

Among the immediate practical tasks you will need to undertake is the gathering together of email addresses, keeping up-to-date address books and mailing lists. As soon as integration work begins, the lists that you and your opposite number have will begin to be out of date, and you need to make sure you develop a system to keep them updated as announcements are made.

It usually takes some time for email addresses to be unified; at this stage all you need to worry about is making sure that, one way or another, you have accurate lists for the various categories of employee.

Noticeboards

Noticeboards can be extremely effective channels of communication if you are looking simply for speed. To manage them properly you need to:

- make sure they are conveniently located for people doing the full range of jobs;

- have special places on them reserved for urgent announcements;

- have someone at each location responsible for putting up notices promptly and taking them down again when appropriate. This person needs to be on the alert for notices, and there needs to be a system in place to cover for their absence. Usually they can be sent the notices by email;

- make sure they are backed up as soon as possible by richer channels where people have a chance to ask questions and where the relevance of the material can be explained.

Telephoning Individuals

If there is a danger that people will hear important announcements affecting them through the grapevine before you have a chance to communicate, you may need to arrange for them to be telephoned at home. To make this work effectively you need to:

- have a system whereby you know who is going to telephone whom. The most likely people to need ringing are:

    - shift workers who are on shifts such as continental shifts, which mean they may not be coming in to work for 24 hours or more after the announcement;

    - people out on the road, for example, service repair or sales people;

    - people on maternity leave or long-term sick leave.

- ensure, where possible, it is immediate managers who make the call;

- give the managers notice if possible of when the announcement will be ready so that they can clear the time to make the calls;

- give the managers a script so that they are consistent and make the main points;

- make sure the text includes how the recipient will hear more and what the channels are for them to put forward questions or points;

- follow-up immediately with written communication so that people can check facts and absorb them in their own time.

Use of Customised Portals

It can be possible to have the new intranet up and running very quickly. Typically organisations manage to have something there by Day One, and gradually over the coming months migrate material from the old intranets.

Team Briefing

If the organisation has an established system of team briefing it can be immensely useful, giving people both the big picture and relating it to the local team. The better systems will also have provision for gathering feedback, which can also be invaluable at this time.

If you do not already have a system in place it is probably not realistic to set one up during the first 100 days. If it works well in one part of the organisation but not the other you may need to build extra channels there to compensate, such as putting the "core" briefs on the intranet and making sure managers have a channel to ask questions so that they can inform their teams.

KEY PLAYERS

Following the deal the emphasis moves from external advisers to the new top team. They will need to establish their identities among the workforce and it is your task to present them.

Especially if there is a major integration programme and many job losses, the HR director is likely to be a key person at this stage of the new organisation. You need to stay close to him or her, as many of the messages which matter most to people are HR ones: pensions, redundancy pay-offs, grades or salary bands for new jobs, responsibilities for new teams, and so on.

WHAT SORT OF LISTENING TO DO AT THIS STAGE

During the first 100 days there are bound to be many individual issues that people want to raise, concerning their future employment prospects, pensions, nature of the work, and so on. The natural person with whom to raise these concerns, a line manager, is likely to be worried about their own position, not to know the answers and, possibly, to move jobs in this period. It is therefore essential that, working with your HR colleagues, you provide employees with one-to-one communication channels so that they can express their concerns and have confidential talks about their personal position. In the absence of anyone able to give time and a genuine listening ear, employees' anger or frustration will increase. You would also find that other channels you set up for upward communication will become clogged with these issues.

You will need to carry out validation, for example to check that particular messages get across, but in the first 100 days will not have time for true evaluation.

It is also important in these first 100 days to understand how people are feeling and what they are thinking. Focus groups, telephone surveys and random face-to-face surveys are all useful methods at this stage.

WHAT EMPLOYEES ARE THINKING AND SAYING

What You Want Them to be Saying

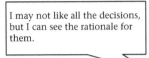

I may not like all the decisions, but I can see the rationale for them.

There's a lot of change, but at least I know who my boss is, and what my priorities are for today.

What You Don't Want Them to be Saying

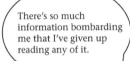

There's so much information bombarding me that I've given up reading any of it.

Have you hear how they treated poor old so-and-so. It just shows that they only care about money.

I'm really worried that I won't be able to keep my shift pattern, but I don't know who to ask about it.

THE COST OF GETTING IT WRONG

The first 100 days are particularly important for setting people's attitudes towards the new organisation. If they decide in these vital days that the organisation is uncaring or inefficient, it will take many years of work to change these views.

A Watson Wyatt survey of 1998–9 showed that although respondents listed effective communication as the second most important contributor to successful M&A, only 4 per cent gave it top priority. The experience most of your employees have had if they have worked in other organisations is therefore likely to be poor, and you should not feel too bad if there are some shortcomings with the effects of your work.

Marks and Mirvis (1986) identified "merger syndrome" as having the following characteristics:

- deteriorating communication;
- poor productivity;
- increasing parochialism;

- power struggles;

- reduced commitment to corporate goals;

- tendency to leave the organisation;

These are likely to be the results if you fail in your work.

SUMMARY FOR INTERNAL COMMUNICATORS

1. Keep the rationale clear and in front of people so that they do not forget the big picture in the welter of other information.

2. Keep reference information about structure and appointments up to date.

3. Don't drown people in information, especially relating to people and parts of the organisation distant from themselves.

4. Make sure you have listening channels in place so that you know who has what concerns or questions. Even if you do not have the answers it is important that people know you are listening.

6 Stage Six: Establishing an Employer Brand for the Merged Organisation

Having made the big announcements about structure, management appointments and locations, you are now ready to move from short-term mode to building an ongoing communication platform. Of course, change has not ceased. Regardless of the merger there are bound to be ongoing structural changes, closures and launches as your organisation grasps opportunities or is hit by failures.

It is not the purpose of this book to offer a blueprint for internal communication in a steady-state organisation. But, as we have already indicated, internal communication has three tasks: communicating the external context in which the organisation works; communication about news and change; and communication about the sort of organisation it is and seeks to become. It is part of your role not only to explain change and its context but to contribute to giving an employee a sense of the distinctive organisation of which they are now a part.

One word of warning: do not try to romance the future for people who are still uncertain about the present – namely their jobs, their location, their terms and conditions, and reporting lines. By all means get agreement to an employer brand project and start thinking about the actions at a senior level, but it should not be announced until the majority of employees in the combined business know the facts one way or the other about themselves and their future.

This chapter deals with the part of your job which concerns the establishment and management of an employer brand, defined by Ambler and Barrow in 1996 as *the package of functional, economic and psychological benefits provided by employment and identified with the employing company.* In any organisation, in particular one which has seen the tensions and stress of a merger or acquisition, it is critical to bring the coherence, direction and focus of brand management to your people.

We will look first at the reasons for establishing an employer brand and then at how to do it. Lastly, we will look at what you must do when there is no need to create a new employer brand, for example in the case of an acquisition of a small company by a much larger one.

WHAT ARE THE BENEFITS OF TAKING AN EMPLOYER BRAND APPROACH?

Employer brand management doesn't replace anything you're doing well already. It simply brings it all together to greater effect, just as consumer brand management has been successfully applied to building brand reputation and winning the commitment and loyalty of customers for over 70 years. As many companies are beginning to realise, the "joined-up" discipline of brand management can equally be applied to attracting, retaining and engaging your most valued employees (from your top "strategic" talent to your front-line "brand ambassadors").

The basic thinking behind employer brand management is that the employee's experience needs to be managed as carefully as that of the customer. Without careful management, the wide variety of experiences that the employee receives before and during employment will give a series of mixed messages and fail to present a coherent picture with which an employee can identify emotionally or intellectually.

The benefits of employer brand management broadly fall into four categories:

1. It is easier to recruit the talent you need. People want to work for an organisation with a good reputation as an employer.

2. It is easier to keep the talent you need as you have been able to match people's own preferences and aspirations with the employment offer and experience.

3. It is easier to elicit high performance from people who are engaged in an organisation which meets their needs.

4. It is easier to be confident that employees are delivering to customers the brand experience that your business success requires.

Several studies have provided evidence that well-managed employer brands lead to organisational success includes.

UK Institute of Employment Studies (1999)

Research conducted with a British retailer established a clear link between staff commitment, customer loyalty and sales growth. Research was conducted among 65,000 employees and 25,000 customers in almost 100 stores. They found that an increase of one point in employee commitment scores (on a five-point scale) represented a 9 per cent increase in monthly sales per store.

Watson Wyatt – Work USA study (1998–2000)

Research sampling 7,500 employees across a wide range of different businesses found a correlation between employee commitment and three-year shareholder return, as shown in Table 6.1.

Table 6.1 **Relationship between employee commitment and shareholder return**

Employee commitment	Return to shareholders
Low	76%
Average	90%
High	112%

Source: Watson Wyatt – Work USA study (1998–2000).

Gallup Retail Study (2000)

Over the last ten years Gallup's Q12 Workplace Survey, which asks 12 key questions linked to employee engagement, has been applied to millions of employees around the world. A study in 2000 aggregating the results from retail companies revealed that the 25 per cent of companies with the highest employee engagement scores enjoy customer-satisfaction levels 39 per cent above average, and have profits 27 per cent higher than average.

International Survey Research (2002)

International Survey Researcher's (ISR) study of over 360,000 employees from the world's ten largest economies showed that net profit margin rose by 2.06 per cent in businesses where employees viewed the business favourably. Companies with less committed employees saw net profit margin fall by 1.38 per cent. The three-year linkage study covered 41 global companies, which had a total of 363,000 employees in 60 countries. The results demonstrated a strong relationship between levels of employee engagement and changes in operating margins. On average, those organisations with high levels of employee engagement increased their operating margins by 3.74 per cent over the three-year period. In those organisations with low levels of engagement, operating margins declined by an average 2.01 per cent over the same period (see Figure 6.1).

The case, then, for taking the trouble to establish and manage a clear employer brand is strong.

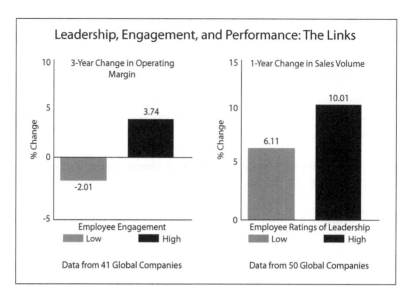

Figure 6.1 **The link between engagement, employee rating of leadership and business performance**

Source: ISR.

HOW TO CREATE AN EMPLOYER BRAND

Here are ten ingredients for employer brand (EB) success:

1. Realisation that achieving an effective EB will need a coherent effort by the whole management team – it should not be seen as the responsibility of only one department, for example HR. While one group may coordinate, the thrust must be a broad one.

2. The overt commitment and continuing involvement of the chairman/ CEO is key. He or she must feel that it is their project. Of course they will be asked to approve any such an initiative but that is not enough. They must be there at the end of each stage and the EB must be firmly on their radar.

3. There must be clear business issues, ideally well quantified, which can be understood by all as the focus for the initial employer brand project. In a merger or acquisition this may mean the retention and motivation of key employee groups, the ability to manage uncomfortable change while maintaining morale, and the restructuring of departments and functions without reducing customer-service standards.

4. An employer brand is not just for Christmas! It is an ongoing approach to the identity and the management of the desired working experience for your people and your management. Procter & Gamble has been running a brand management system for its consumer brands since 1931 and brand management shows no sign of flagging as an approach.

5.	There is no off-the-peg, standard EB. The EB you need is the one which will deliver the relevant working experience which will recruit, retain and engage the people you need to achieve your business objectives. There is no need to ape so-called best practice. Indeed your EB should be a beacon for what is special about you. As Michael Porter (1980) says, what you decide *not* to do is as important as what you say you *will* do.

6.	Your EB must reflect the reality of the working experience, including all the elements which create that (and which we will cover later in this chapter). Again, what you major on will be a function of your circumstances and needs. You cannot spin your way to an employer brand, and it may be necessary to make important and hard changes to achieve what you aspire to.

7.	Those hard changes may well include changes to the way the board and the senior executives actually behave. Unless this happens projects will rarely be successful. You will need to have courage and a powerful argument.

8.	Follow a clear road map which will ensure that the steps on the journey are all followed. A critical early action, after senior management commitment, is to form a working group which will include HR, Marketing, Corporate Communications and a senior line manager.

9.	Establish a rough cost of the whole EB development exercise, including agreeing the plan internally, winning approval more broadly, conducting relevant employee research, establishing the need for specific changes to the working experience, managing the communication and launch needs. It is worth sketching out the resource implications.

10.	It can be worth using a specialist consultant who knows both EB and M&A. All major transactions will, of course, use accountants and many of these have consulting arms that can handle the so-called "soft issues" and offer a one stop shop. However, you may find that two specialists is a better option, since the specialist employer brand providers may be able to take a stronger line on people and communication issues than consultants concentrating mainly on cost synergies or IT projects.

These are the key ingredients; now what are the detailed steps which will take you through an EB project if followed successfully?

The following road map draws on the experience of many of the leading thinkers and practitioners in this fast-developing management approach. It aims to provide a practical step-by-step guide to developing and implementing an EB strategy that not only delivers on your immediate business objectives, but also helps to ensure your EB is built to last.

Step 1: Clarify Your Desired Destination

To clarify your desired destination you need to address the question: where are you trying to take the business, and how can a stronger employer brand help you to get there?

To answer this question, you will need to clarify:

• the business goals (short-term imperatives and long-term vision);

• the potential role of people management in achieving these goals;

• the current EB strengths you can leverage;

• the current EB weaknesses you need to address to contribute more effectively to the success of the business.

Step 2: Clarify Where You Can and Can't Go

If your company forms part of a wider corporate entity, you will need to clarify the scope you have for local EB development. Even if there is no corporate level EB strategy, it is likely that there will be a number of corporate parameters within which you will need to work. These may include a common statement of purpose and values, identity guidelines, operating principles and shared services. If there is some form of overall employer brand strategy, you can still add value by tailoring this strategy to your local needs.

Table 6.2   Different business needs and the benefits of a strong employer brand

Business need	Specific benefit of strong EB
Business is trying to build competitive differentiation in the marketplace by offering a distinctive style of service	Helps to promote brand advocacy and the right kind of behaviour change among employees
Business is striving to build new capabilities	Helps you to attract and retain the right kind of talent
Business is trying to complete a merger or acquisition	Helps to forge a common sense of purpose and identity, and ease the process of assimilation
Business is striving to retain a distinctive culture as it matures	Provides a mechanism for "bottling" the winning spirit that is too often lost as companies grow in size and complexity

How can you create brand consistency and alignment without succumbing to bland uniformity?

Even the most carefully managed global brands, like Coca-Cola, have gone "glocal" to meet the specific needs of their local markets. Brand consistency provides a powerful advantage in clarifying the brand message, but only up to a point. If brands don't resonate with their local markets, consistency counts for nothing. This is just as true for EB management as it is for the customer-facing brand. Where there are two levels of branding, the general rule is to align the EB with the customer-facing brand to ensure integrity between the internal and external faces of the brand. You may need to take the following steps:

1. clarify which corporate elements need to be explicitly incorporated into your local EB proposition;

2. identify the parameters you need to work within (such as identity guidelines);

3. clarify the core values of your customer brand proposition;

4. determine the degree of freedom you have in tailoring your proposition to employees and the local labour market.

Where multi-branded businesses share a corporate management development programme, there may be a requirement for a two-tier employer brand model.

Regional differences in the labour market and the cultural expectations of employees may require a degree of local tailoring to the employer brand.

Step 3: Join Up Your Thinking

In our experience, few EB development projects are successful without close coordination between the HR, marketing, corporate communications and line management functions.

How can you find the best way to help each other?

In a recent workshop, representatives from a range of leading companies identified the areas in which each function could add most value to the EB development process (see Figure 6.2).

Once you have identified the mutual benefits of developing an EB strategy, we would recommend that you set up a steering group comprising representatives from each function to guide the following steps in the process.

This is seen as a commercial initiative, led by HR and supported and endorsed by marketing. Using marketing techniques to develop the people brand has forced us to use the kind of business language that hasn't previously been part of our lexicon.

Tom Brown, HRD Allied-Domecq, following
an employer brand programme.

Marketing	Line Management
External brand requirements	Needs "on the ground"
Research and analysis	Practical implementation
Brand activation "tools"	Political "savvy"

Human Resources	Internal Communications
Recruitment	Understanding the audience
Performance managment	Engagement
Reward and recognition	"Air traffic control"

Figure 6.2   How different functions add value to employer brand development projects

Source: People in Business.

Step 4: Establish Your Business Case

Typically, in any M&A transaction, there will need to be consideration of the people aspects of both companies, assuming that the plan is to merge them to achieve the necessary synergies. This will cover the terms and conditions of each group of employees, including basic pay, bonuses/profit sharing, holidays, notice periods and, of course, pensions. If there is union involvement a plan will be necessary for their involvement.

These dimensions are all important EB considerations but working through them does not mean you will necessarily emerge with the right result. Creating the effective "best of both" out of each side and then making the leap towards something which unites, inspires and acts as a guide for all people-related actions is a much bigger undertaking because it will force discussion on much broader subjects than the basics.

It is impossible to develop an effective long-term EB strategy without a clear mandate and proactive support from the senior team. An EB strategy relies heavily on HR to shape the promise and many of the deliverables, but without support from the top it is unlikely to carry the authority or attract the resources required to give the EB proposition real substance.

Checklist: Securing senior management involvement and support

• Frame the EB strategy in terms that the CEO and management board will recognise.

• Lobby in advance to identify whom you can count on for support, and the most likely objections and counter-arguments.

- Identify the challenges that the strategy will help you to address (for example, poor external image, difficulty in attracting talent, low employee morale, poor retention).

- Demonstrate how the strategy links into the overall business plan, and will help to meet goals and targets.

- Explain how it will complement (and help to coordinate) the other HR, marketing and communications initiatives that are already in progress.

- Provide benchmark evidence identifying how this approach has benefited other companies (particularly your competitors).

- Make a realistic assessment of what you hope to achieve in terms of cost savings or added value, and identify the metrics you will use to measure success.

- Clarify the investment in time and money required to deliver the strategy and your expected return on investment.

- Dramatise the benefits of success (even the most hard-nosed investment decision involves an element of "gut feel" and emotional engagement).

Step 5: Build a Brand Insight Platform

Great brands are founded on and sustained by great insights. While brand image and customer-satisfaction surveys bear some resemblance to employee surveys, there is a wide array of other methodologies and techniques used by marketing departments which could equally be applied to exploring employees' perceptions of the brand that they work for.

Checklist: Questions to help you establish employee perceptions of your current employer brand

- How do employees currently view your EB? (If your employees are asked to describe the kind of organisation they work for, how are they likely to reply?)

- Do people have a strong sense of the organisation's purpose and values (both implicit and explicit)? Is there a consistent core of opinion shared by all employees?

- What behaviours are felt to be most characteristic of the organisation? What are the "moments of truth" when your organisation is at its best (and worse)?

- What currently drives people's commitment and what demoralises people?

- Why do people choose to join the organisation and why do they leave? (This may be a critical question if you need to rebuild your management team.)

- Are you sure that you are tapping into enough sources of potential insight to get a fully rounded picture?

Step 6: Define Your Employer Brand Promise

One of the key differences between a brand and a product is focus. Volkswagen has a wide range of models, each offering hundreds of features, but the key to the brand for many years has been the notion of reliability. Brands help people to distinguish what makes you special, and provide a clear reason for people to commit to a brand relationship. There is no single formula for a winning brand proposition, but it should be single-minded. It could focus on the quality of your products and services, the distinctive package of employee benefits you offer, the values that underpin your company culture, or a big idea that inspires your purpose and direction.

What benefits do you want people to associate with you as an employer?

- Can you translate the customer brand promise directly into something that will be relevant and compelling to employees?

- Is there a big idea that inspires the purpose and direction of the company?

- Have you identified the main drivers of employee recruitment and commitment? Is there a unifying theme that could provide you with a focal point?

- Is *what* you do more likely to provide a distinctive focus, or *how* you do it?

- In which areas could you most credibly demonstrate a clear competitive edge?

- Could you leverage your corporate branding to greater effect?

- Which of the answers to the above is most compelling and credible?

Examples of employer brand propositions

Tesco maintains that its brand proposition – "Every little helps" – works just as well with employees as customers. Translated internally it is associated with an openness to new ideas, and a constant stream of initiatives designed to make jobs more interesting and rewarding.

Car maker Ford found that the primary source of employee motivation was great enthusiasm for the type of work they are involved in, so the focus of Ford's employer brand proposition is "Natural passion".

Alongside the status appeal of their brands in the marketplace, companies like Sky and Microsoft have focused on people's potential to develop and progress within the company, an approach that has enabled them to "select the very best from the talent pool available".

Unilever has begun to leverage the strengths and opportunities associated with its corporate brand to improve the appeal of its individually branded operating companies.

Step 7: Define your Brand Promise

The brand positioning statement provides the principal navigational tool for brand planning, clarifying the focal points for developing and managing the brand experience.

Most brand positioning models ignore the employee dimension, despite the fact that it is clear that employees experience the brand in a different way from the customer, and are motivated by different types of benefit. The model shown in Figure 6.3 presents a more integrated approach. To ensure brand integrity it recognises that some brand qualities need to shine through every stakeholder's experience of the brand, while others need to be specifically designed to meet the more specific needs and aspirations of customers and employees.

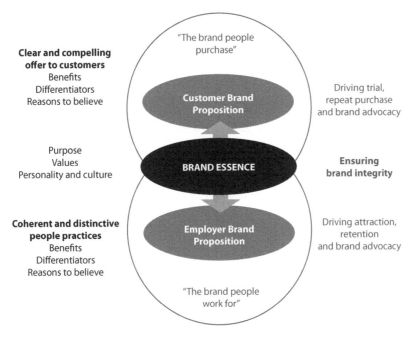

Figure 6.3   Integrated brand positioning model

Source: People in Business.

The most difficult qualities to identify are the brand "differentiators" (what makes you different? what is your competitive edge?) and "reasons to believe" (what are the tangible ways in which the benefits and differentiators are demonstrated? how are these promises embedded in people's experience of the brand?). While the brand positioning statement provides a focal point for action, it should not be regarded as static. A strong brand essence should endure over time, but the benefits, differentiators and reasons to believe are likely to require constant refreshment to maintain competitive advantage.

Step 8: Tailoring Your Proposition

It is not untypical for brands to encompass a wide range of different products and services. Think of Virgin. Virgin's essence is all about being "for the people and against the big guy", which generally translates into being good value, down to earth and fun. Within this brand umbrella it has successfully offered music, transatlantic flights and financial services. While few brands are as elastic as Virgin, this demonstrates the point that once you have a big employer brand idea (your core proposition), you still have plenty of leeway for tailoring what you offer to specific target groups, as long as you are clear about what they all share in common.

How do you maintain employer brand consistency without limiting your flexibility to attract and retain different types of employee?

This is clearly an important consideration for your EB strategy, because with many different types of employee to cater for (according to level, function, and so on) you will need to offer more than "one size fits all" to compete in the job market and to grow and keep the different kinds of people you need. These tailored "packages" are generally described as targeted value propositions (or TVPs).

Employer brand strategies generally encompass some form of employee segmentation, both internally, among current employees, and externally, for important sectors of the labour market (such as graduates or specific skill groups). The brand strategy needs to clarify:

- how far it is acceptable to go before you overstep the overall brand promise?

- how you can ensure that every TVP incorporates common brand attribute?

A number of organisations segment their employees according to whether the psychological contract with the employer is primarily "transactional" (good pay and rations) or "relational" (values and status driven).

Step 9: Employer Brand Identity

Branding is too often misinterpreted as little more than the creation of a
new brand name, logo and design scheme (the look and feel of the brand).
Presentation is important, but a smart brand "wrapper' will soon be exposed if
there is little substance to the underlying experience.

Having made this essential point, if the underlying quality of your employer
offering is sound, then the creation of a more consistent internal brand
identity can play an important role in improving people's perceptions of what
you have to offer.

How can you ensure coherent expression of the employer brand?

- Work within existing brand identity guidelines.

- Create a consistent look and feel for everything you produce
  internally that supports the EB offer (from pension policy documents
  to newsletters).

- Rationalise the separate sub-identities used for departments,
  management initiatives, shared services and communication
  channels that often confuse efforts to create a coherent employer
  brand experience.

- Don't confuse the creation of a consistent EB identity with branding
  the HR function. While HR plays a central role in employer brand
  management, there is clearly more to the employer brand experience
  than HR.

- Avoid creating a look and feel for your internal communication of
  the EB that gives the impression that it is no more than a short-term
  campaign initiative.

Barclays realised that one of the reasons that its employees were undervaluing the
total sum of the benefits that they were offered as employees was because they
were being communicated in a confusing multiplicity of different formats. When
they began to package these benefits more consistently, from the new company
pension scheme to the innovative Barclays University, employee perceptions of
the Barclays employer brand showed significant improvement.

Step 10: Coherent Delivery

It is often mistakenly assumed that the first stage of implementation should
be some form of brand engagement programme. In our experience this often
promotes greater cynicism than brand advocacy. Our recommendation would
be to focus on making sure that product and service improvements are in
place first before any mass communication to employees is contemplated.

How can you ensure coherent delivery of the employer brand?

The marketing concept of the brand mix (incorporating all of the controllable elements that contribute towards people's experience of a brand) is just as useful to apply internally as externally. From this perspective your internal communication represents only one aspect of the EB mix that you may need to address.

While the exact constituents of the mix will vary from company to company, the Figure 6.4 provides an illustration of the typical elements.

Figure 6.4   Typical constituents of the employer brand mix

Source: People in Business.

Step 11: Communication

As the internal communicator you are likely to have been involved as a member of the core team delivering all of the above steps. Step 11 is clearly particularly relevant to you.

While mass communication to all employees is unlikely to be effective until the EB mix has been aligned with the desired promise, some form of management brief will clearly be necessary at an early stage to clarify the rationale for change. Depending on how much change is required of managers themselves, this may require some form of engagement or learning exercise to elicit their support and clarify what is expected of them.

What is the best way to communicate the employer brand?

- Applying brand thinking and marketing tools does not mean you need to use brand jargon in your communication. It's no more relevant to your employees than to your customers. You should focus on the benefits not the underlying methodology.

- Avoid the temptation to over-claim for dramatic effect. To ensure that your communication is credible, it's better to focus on what is already on offer, or soon to be available, rather than focus on a utopian vision that feels far removed from current reality.

- Don't forget that your external communication (including recruitment and consumer advertising) can also send powerful messages to your employees about the kind of organisation you are, or claim to be. Make sure your employees feel the promise is credible, rather than risk over-promising to customers or new recruits.

- Take the long-term view and be careful not to position employer branding as a campaign initiative. You wouldn't succeed in the marketplace by treating your external brand communication as a short-term initiative; by the same standards, you shouldn't expect to succeed in building a strong employer brand by putting all your emphasis on a Big Bang launch and then neglecting to follow through.

- Recognise that from the employee's perspective, all your internal communication has the potential to reinforce or undermine how people feel about the company. You're unlikely to build trust and credibility in your EB unless you deliver a degree of consistency across all of your communications.

- Don't forget the "body language" of the organisation. People pay far more attention to what is done than what is said. Look for ways of symbolising your intent through tangible actions, including attention to managers who feel that, as successful business "operators", they are exempt from the brand values (see box).

Importance of communicating internal brand messages

Recently there have been advertising campaigns by a number of organisations portraying their employees as smiley, happy people devoted to serving the customer's every whim. In at least one case there has been no corresponding internal communication or support to help front-line employees live up to these promises, resulting in an unsurprising deterioration in employee relations.

The BBC uses what it calls a "story wheel" to map out its internal brand messages; an approach which it believes has contributed significantly to an improvement in employee perceptions.

A recent client claimed that downgrading the status of a manager who had been flagrantly ignoring the company's stated values was worth at least £50,000 worth of internal communication claiming the values were important.

Step 12: Employer Brand Management

After the excitement of the development and launch phases has subsided, keeping employer brand issues on the agenda can feel like hard uphill work.

How do you maintain continuity and keep on track?

In our experience there are three essential steps you need to take to keep up the momentum:

1. Develop a five-year plan for your EB, which aligns with the long-term goals of the business. This should include:

    –   immediate steps you can take to package what you currently do well more effectively;

    –   a two- to three-year plan, which should aim to address your main weaknesses and build on your strengths;

    –   a longer-term vision, which sets out your more aspirational objectives for building EB leadership.

2. Establish clear accountability and a clear process for coordinating all of the activities that will impact on the EB (not just recruitment or internal communication). This will generally require close cooperation between the CEO, HR director, marketing director and the director responsible for internal communications, and possibly the appointment of a full-time employer brand manager.

3. A regular review of progress versus objectives and the refinement or restructuring of activities that appear to be under-delivering.

It is vital that you find the right person for the role of EB manager. As with their colleagues in consumer goods they should already be potential senior managers, although the line management power they have will be limited. This is a job where influence based on knowledge is more important. Some experience across different disciplines is also critical, with a combination of HR and marketing experience being the ideal. In our view the incumbent should report to the HR director while having close links across the organisation, including with the most senior management.

Step 13: Measure Your Progress

There has been a growing focus on the measurement of employee commitment over recent years, and many of the top employee research firms can offer sophisticated analyses of the underlying factors that drive commitment to the organisation. There have also been some significant developments in the measurement of the "service profit chain", which seeks to track the relationship between employee commitment to the organisation, customer satisfaction and bottom-line profitability.

Research has demonstrated that employers which attract high levels of employee commitment can be associated over time with:

- higher levels of customer satisfaction (Gallup);

- higher profit margins (ISR);

- higher shareholder returns (Watson Wyatt).

League tables of the best employers, derived from standardised employee survey questionnaires, have also become popular in recent years. These include the *Financial Times* "Best Places to Work" (UK and Europe) and *The Sunday Times* "Best Companies to Work For" (UK).

> Since Sainsburys embarked on its new employer brand strategy in 2001 (which included the appointment of its first employer brand manager) employee turnover has fallen significantly, saving the company millions of pounds, and its position in *The Times'* Top 100 Graduate Employers has improved from 67th to 18th.

The EB manager should, of course, regularly monitor all the internal HR measures, for example:

- staff turnover by location, seniority and skill area;

- results of exit interviews;

- appraisal results, in that they have taken place and what average ratings have been given;

- the ratio of acceptances to offers made in recruitment;

- attitudes of applicants rejected by the company at the end of the recruitment process;

- attitudes of alumni (your company should be a springboard for career growth whether people stay or go – that is one of the reasons people will join you and you should be able to celebrate your alumni's achievements for that reason);

- employee research trends on job satisfaction, recognition and many other dimensions;

- sickness/absence trends by location and function;

- diversity profile (gender, age, race, ethnicity and sexual orientation is also measured in many organisations);

- the extent to which these HR measures feature in internal and particularly in management communications.

It should be the EB manager's role to influence senior management so that the condition of the EB is as closely measured and studied. In the delicate months after a merger or acquisition this is a vital part of the process.

WHEN THERE IS NO NEED TO CREATE A NEW EMPLOYER BRAND

You may not, in fact, need a new EB. There are several circumstances where this will be the case. If, for example, the acquisition is simply the adding of assets, distribution capability or plant then the bidder's existing EB should be maintained. You do not need another one. EasyJet's acquisition of GB Airways in 2007 is an example of this. The deal provides attractive routes, good people and aircraft, but the size of the deal for the acquirer does not justify a change to the latter's established culture, structure and identity. Management behaviours and communications should, of course, be sensitive to the need to welcome new people – being bought does not mean that the individuals are less valuable and they will need to be inspired by the promise of the new and larger company and their prospects.

Another case where a new EB may not be desirable is when the deal concentrates on buying an existing and well-regarded business which is very different to the acquirer's business. The acquired brand will have its own style, its own management and its own customers and the last thing it will want is a new owner cutting across well-established relationships with people they trust. For years this was the successful strategy for Whitbread Group, which made well-judged acquisitions and joint ventures like Costa Coffee, TGI Fridays and Pizza Hut among others. While financial, legal and compliance needs will have to impact any new acquisition, those interventions should not interfere with a good idea and an existing employer brand which has already made an impact.

Sometimes, at group level, the brand is limited to being an owner with no trading responsibilities. A master of deal-making on these lines is Sir Martin Sorrell's WPP, owner of numerous outstanding companies in the advertising and communications world like JWT, Ogilvy and Young and Rubicam. Interference with the employer brands of those organisations, which are largely dependent on the skills and emotions of people who chose to join one of them (not some great group), would risk destroying value. Interestingly, the pressure for global coordination is causing WPP to be involved in something that I am sure they did not plan, namely the pitching for global business, led by WPP, with a service offering including several of the independent companies working together.

KEY PLAYERS

- Marketing people, especially those concerned with the brand, who will be key stakeholders with whom you will need to work closely.

- HR will have a lead role to play in delivering many of the policy aspects of the new employer brand and you will need to work closely with them.

- Learning and development people specifically who will have a role in ensuring managers are able to play their part.

- Line managers who deliver most of the actual day-to-day practice and culture that play an important part in the EB.

WHAT SORT OF LISTENING YOU NEED TO DO AT THIS STAGE

- Naturally there is a lot of listening to do in the insight phase to make sure that you design an EB which meets employees' various needs as well as those of the business.

- With the new company up and running you will need to devise ways of regularly both listening to and measuring employees' views on your delivery on the EB.

WHAT EMPLOYEES ARE THINKING AND SAYING

What You Want Them to be Thinking and Saying

I'm so glad I stayed with the Group and didn't take voluntary redundancy.

This is a place that really understands what I need from them to work well – and delivers it.

This is an organisation that knows where it's going, and I want to go there with it.

What You Don't Want Them to be Thinking and Saying

> You wouldn't believe what a mess we are in. I can't stand the stress and I'm looking for another job.

> Oh, for the good old days with [former employer].

> They just don't care about me.

THE COST OF GETTING IT WRONG

- Failing to establish an EB once the dust has settled following a merger or acquisition can mean that employees carry with them out-of-date expectations from their former parts of the organisation.

- There can also be poor relations between people at every level as a "them and us" attitude prevents smooth working across teams or in mixed teams. This can hamper potential efficiency gains.

- There is a mass of evidence suggesting a high turnover of people, especially managers, from newly acquired companies. Replacing these people is not just expensive in recruitment costs but also in lost expertise.

SUMMARY FOR INTERNAL COMMUNICATORS

1. Work with colleagues to establish a clear employer brand for the new organisation.

2. Be clear about how to demonstrate it in the range of communication that you are responsible for, both in terms of content and channels.

3. Make sure that you reflect the employer brand in the tone and channels as well as the content of any material you are responsible for.

Bibliography

Aiello, R.J. and Watkins, M.D. (2000), "The Fine Art of Friendly Acquisition" HBR Nov–Dec.

Allee, V. (2003), *The Future of Knowledge* (Oxford: Butterworth Heinemann).

Ambler, T. and Barrow, S. (1996), "The Employer Brand", *Journal of Brand Management* 4:3.

Ashkenas, R.N. and Francis, S.C. (2000), "Integration Managers: Special Leaders for Special Times", HBR Nov–Dec.

Ashkenas, R.N., Demonaco, L.J. and Francis, S.C. (1998), "Making the Deal Real: How GE Capital Integrates Acquisitions", HBR Jan–Feb.

Cabrera, J.C. (1986), "The Human Resource Side of Mergers and Acquisitions: Potential Costs and Benefits", *Asset Based Financial Journal* 7, 27–30.

Carey, D. (2000), "A CEO Roundtable on Making Mergers Succeed" HBR May–June.

Covello, V.T., Peters, Richard G., Wojtecki, J.G. and Hyde, R.C. (2001), "Risk Communication, the West Nile Virus Epidemic, and Bioterrorism: Responding to the Communication Challenges Posed by the Intentional or Unintentional Release of a Pathogen in an Urban Setting", *Journal of Urban Health: Bulletin of the New York Academy of Medicine* 78:2, 382–391.

Cliffe, S. (1999), "Can this Merger be Saved?", HBR Jan–Feb.

Clutterbuck, D. and Hirst, S. (2003), *Talking Business* (Oxford: Butterworth Heinemann).

The Conference Board *Employee Communication During Merger. Report No 1270 –00-R.*

Cruise O'Brien, R. (2001), *Trust: Releasing the Energy to Succeed* (Chichester: Wiley).

Devine, M. and Hirsch, W. (1998), *Mergers and Acquisitions: Getting the People Bit Right* (Horsham: Roffey Park).

Devine, Marion (2002), *Successful Mergers* (London: *The Economist*).

Eccles, R.G. and Nohria, N. (1992), *Beyond the Hype: Rediscovering the Essence of Management* (Boston: Harvard Business School Press).

Grundy, T. (2003), *Smart Things to Know about Mergers and Acquisitions* (Oxford: Capstone).

Hanneman, R.A. and Riddle, M. (2005), *Introduction to Social Network Methods* (Riverside, CA: University of California) (published in digital form at http://faculty.ucr.edu/~hanneman/).

Hespeslagh, P.C. and Jemison, D.B. (1991), *Managing Acquisitions* (New York: The Free Press).

Hofstede, G. (2005), *Cultures and Organisations* (London: McGraw Hill).

Hubbard, N. (2001), *Acquisition Strategy and Implementation* (Basingstoke: Palgrave).

Hunt, J. (1987), *Mergers and Acquisitions*. LBS, Egon Zehnder

Lees, S. (2003), *Global Acquisitions* (Basingstoke: Palgrave).

Light, D. (2001), "Who Goes, Who Stays?", HBR Jan.

Magnet, M. (1984), "Acquiring without Smothering", *Fortune* 1984:22.

Marks, M.L., and Mirvis, P. (1986), "The Merger Syndrome", *Psychology Today* Oct, 36–42.

Mitchell, D. and Holmes, G., (1996) *Making Acquisitions Work: Learning from Companies' Successes and Failures* (London: Research report).

Porter, M.E. (1980), *Competitive Strategy* (New York: The Free Press).

Quirke, B. (1995), *Communicating Change* (Berkshire: McGraw Hill).

Quirke, B. (2000), *Making the Connections: Using Internal Communication to Turn Strategy into Action* (Hampshire: Gower).

Schein, E.H. (1996), *Organisational Culture and Leadership,* (San Francisco: Jossey-Bass).

Scholes, E. (ed.) (1997), *Gower Handbook of Internal Communication* (Aldershot: Gower).

Schmidt, J.A. (2002), *Making Mergers Work: The Strategic Importance of People* (Alexandria, VA: SHRM).

Taffinder, P. (1999), *Big Change: Route Map for Corporate Transformation* (New York: Wiley).

Trompenaars, F. and Hampden-Turner, C. (1997), *Riding the Waves of Culture* (London: Nicholas Brealey).

Walsh, J.P. (1988), "Top Management Turnover Following Mergers and Acquisitions", *Strategic Management Journal* 9, 173–183.

Wenger, E. (1999), *Communities of Practice, Learning, Meaning and Identity* (Cambridge: Cambridge University Press).

Wishard, B.J. (1985), "The Human Dimension", *The Magazine Bank Administration*, 61:6, 74–79.

Index